Electric Cars

OTHER TITLES IN THE TECHNOLOGY 360 SERIES:

Electric Cars

Jenny MacKay

LUCENT BOOKS
A part of Gale, Cengage Learning

GALE
CENGAGE Learning™

Detroit • New York • San Francisco • New Haven, Conn • Waterville, Maine • London

LIBRARY OF CONGRESS CATALOGING-IN-PUBLICATION DATA

MacKay, Jenny, 1978-
    Electric Cars / by Jenny MacKay.
        p. cm. — (Technology 360)
    Includes bibliographical references and index.
    ISBN 978-1-4205-0612-9 (hardback)
    1. Electric automobiles—Juvenile literature. I. Title.
    TL220.M27 2011
    629.22'93--dc23
    2011016597

Lucent Books
27500 Drake Rd
Farmington Hills MI 48331

ISBN-13: 978-1-4205-0612-9
ISBN-10: 1-4205-0612-9

Printed in the United States of America
2 3 4 5 6 7 15 14 13 12 11

CONTENTS

"As we go forward, I hope we're going to continue to use technology to make really big differences in how people live and work."
—Sergey Brin, co-founder of Google

The past few decades have seen some amazing advances in technology. Many of these changes have had a direct and measureable impact on the way people live, work, and play. Communication tools, such as cell phones, satellites, and the Internet, allow people to keep in constant contact across longer distances and from the most remote places. In fields related to medicine, existing technologies—digital imaging devices, robotics and lasers, for example—are being used to redefine surgical procedures and diagnostic techniques. As technology has become more complex, however, so have the related ethical, legal, and safety issues.

Psychologist B.F. Skinner once noted that "the real problem is not whether machines think but whether men do." Recent advances in technology have, in many cases, drastically changed the way people view the world around them. They can have a conversation with someone across the globe at lightning speed, access a huge universe of information with the click of a key, or become an avatar in a virtual world of their own making. While advances like these have been viewed as a great boon in some quarters, they have also opened the door to questions about whether or not the speed of technological advancement has come at an unspoken price. A closer examination of the evolution and use of these devices provides a deeper understanding of the social, cultural and ethical implications that they may hold for our future.

Technology 360 not only explores how evolving technologies work, but also examines the short- and long-term impact of their use on society as a whole. Each volume in Technology 360 focuses on a particular invention, device or family of similar devices, exploring how the device was developed; how it works; its impact on society; and possible future uses. Volumes also contain a chronology specific to each topic, a glossary of technical terms used in the text, and a subject index. Sidebars, photos and detailed illustrations, tables, charts and graphs help further illuminate the text.

Titles in this series emphasize inventions and devices familiar to most readers, such as robotics, digital cameras, iPods, and video games. Not only will users get an easy-to-understand, "nuts and bolts" overview of these inventions, they will also learn just how much these devices have evolved. For example, in 1973 a Motorola cell phone weighed about two pounds and cost $4000.00—today, cell phones weigh only a few ounces and are inexpensive enough for every member of the family to have one. Lasers—long a staple of the industrial world—have become highly effective surgical tools, capable of reshaping the cornea of the eye and cleaning clogged arteries. Early video games were played on large machines in arcades; now, many families play games on sophisticated home systems that allow for multiple players and cross-location networking.

IMPORTANT DATES

1780
Italian physician Luigi Galvani discovers that electric forces have roles in the bodies of living things.

1876
German inventor Nikolaus Otto invents the four-stroke internal combustion engine.

1834
American inventor Thomas Davenport builds the first electric motor.

1884
British inventor Thomas Parker creates a street-sized electric vehicle.

1912
American engineer Charles Kettering creates an electric ignition for internal combustion engines.

1800   **1850**   **1900**

1800
Italian physicist Alessandro Volta creates the Voltaic pile, the first battery.

1859
French physicist Gaston Planté invents the lead acid storage battery.

in the Development of Electric Cars

2010
The mostly electric Chevrolet Volt and the all-electric Nissan LEAF are introduced to American buyers.

1970
The U.S. government enacts the Clean Air Act to limit exhaust emissions from industrial sources and automobiles.

1984
The first 100% solar-powered vehicle is invented.

2000
The first Toyota Prius hybrids are sold in the United States.

1991
Japan begins producing lithium-ion batteries.

1970

1990

2010

1990
The first nickel metal hydride battery is produced commercially.

2010
Honda produces the FCX Clarity, the world's first hydrogen fuel cell vehicle.

Electricity in Motion

The automobile has been part of human life for only about 150 years, merely a sliver of time among thousands of years of recorded human history. Nevertheless, this technological wonder has done much to shape the geography, lifestyle, and politics of the modern human world. When the very first self-propelled vehicles were invented in the mid-1800s, people were a bit wary of them. The public still preferred traveling on foot, on horseback, or in animal-drawn carts and carriages, the way people had been getting around for centuries. By the turn of the twentieth century, however, the self-propelled vehicle, which could be controlled from inside by a driver using foot pedals and a steering wheel, became more than a passing fancy. Its popularity took root, especially in countries like the United States, where cities were growing and people were always looking for new technology and trends. The automobile came to shape the development of the world. It spurred the construction of roads, highways, freeways, and refueling stations in networks that spanned entire continents. The earth's land masses were transformed to make way for a modern human invention now central to the lifestyle of a great many people—the automated vehicle.

At the turn of the twentieth century, these world-changing vehicles were powered by various means. Some contained engines than ran on heat from the burning of fuel. Others had batteries and drove on electrical power. Faced with different options, drivers eventually came to prefer the more powerful heat engines and their readily available fuel: gasoline. In the years since, electric cars have fallen by the wayside, never disappearing but never quite keeping pace with the faster combustion engines, either. The electric car has traveled quieter roads and held quieter jobs, always existing in the shadow of bigger, stronger engines with an appetite for gasoline.

Combustion engines have since made many changes to the world—and not all of these changes have been good. The pollution caused by millions of gasoline-burning cars has clouded once blue skies and could be changing the very climate of our planet. The fuel these cars require also rests in pools deep underground, reached only by drilling and pumping at great human effort and expense—and the supply is not unlimited. In the face of air pollution and the rising cost of gasoline, electric cars have begun to make a comeback. Their batteries are newer and stronger than ever before, and their clean, whisper-quiet engines have been getting the attention of car owners and drivers all around the world. The electric vehicle was widely admired once, at the dawn of the automotive age. After waiting quietly backstage for the past century of automobile history, it may now step out to take a leading role in the car industry once again.

A maze of roads marking interchanges of the highway system are common to the landscape of the United States, where automobiles are a critical part of the economy and culture.

CHAPTER 1

Electric Vehicles, Past to Present

For thousands of years, people have been fascinated by the idea of a naturally occurring and often powerful form of energy known as electricity. Static sparking between pieces of clothing that are rubbed together or hair rising toward the touch of another surface, such as fabric, are intriguing events that human beings have not always understood. Perhaps the most noticeable evidence of the existence of electricity is lightning, a violent, powerful, and potentially destructive force. Several thousand years ago, about 1000 B.C., the phenomenon of lightning was a central part of the ancient Greeks' beliefs about gods. The mightiest god in Greek mythology was Zeus, who wielded the lightning bolt as the most powerful and feared weapon in the heavens.

Electrical energy has done more than shape cultural myths and beliefs over the centuries. It also has inspired curiosity among scientists and inventors who have looked up at the sky during storms and wondered if the power and force of a bolt of lightning could be harnessed somehow for humans to use. Among those who experimented with this idea was American inventor and statesman Benjamin Franklin, who in 1752 flew a kite with a metal key attached to it during a thunderstorm. His goal was to prove that lightning was the same force that occurred in smaller sparks of static electricity he had observed on clothing and hair. Franklin enlisted the help of his 21-year-old son, and they stood outdoors in a thunderstorm flying the kite as near to the clouds as they could. After a long wait, Franklin noticed small threads of the kite's string beginning to stand erect and separate from one another. His theory was that the threads were being energized by electricity traveling down the kite string from the clouds. He reached one of his knuckles up toward the key on the end of the string, and a visible spark of static electricity appeared between the metal and his skin. This indicated the kite had indeed picked up electric energy from the clouds that was carried down the string, to the key, and to an object (in this case a person) on the ground. The spark supported Franklin's theory that lightning was a powerful force of static electricity created in clouds and transferred to Earth's surface. Soon after this experiment, Franklin installed a metal lightning rod on the roof of his house to draw lightning indoors. The rod was connected to two bells threaded on a wire that touched the ground. Whenever an electrical storm occurred, electricity would charge the string to make it twitch, and Franklin's bells would begin to ring. He had succeeded in harnessing electrical energy to *do* something.

Moved by Electricity

Franklin was not the only person interested in the power of electricity. Across the Atlantic Ocean, European scientists formed an active community that studied electric energy, where it came from, and what it might be harnessed to do. These scientists made a series of important discoveries that eventually led to the creation of the first electrically powered vehicle. One significant discovery came about when an Italian physician named Luigi Galvani found that electricity has important roles in the bodies of living things. Galvani was dissecting a frog in 1780 when he noticed that the frog's leg twitched whenever he touched one of its bared nerves with

A lithograph depicts Benjamin Franklin and his son William conducting a now-famous experiment using a kite and a key to prove Franklin's theory that lightning was electricity.

a steel scalpel. Galvani believed that the fluid in the frog's body was generating the electricity. Another Italian scientist who read about Galvani's findings, Alessandro Volta, thought differently. He correctly predicted that the source of the electricity in the dead frog actually came from a chemical reaction that happened when the frog's body fluids were touched by two different types of metal. Volta went on to show that when two different metals were submerged near one another in a liquid solution of acid, or an electrolyte, they generated electricity.

Building on this discovery, Volta tried submerging different kinds of metals into an acidic solution to see what would happen. He found that the metals copper and zinc worked especially well at reacting with one another to create an electrical charge. In 1800, Volta devised a contraption of a series of copper and zinc rings, submerged in acid, that generated a consistent flow of electricity, known as an electrical current. The invention became known as the Voltaic cell or Voltaic pile, but it was actually the first battery. Volta had found a way to turn chemical energy into electrical energy. His discovery at the turn of the nineteenth century is

Ancient Electricity

Italian physicist Alessandro Volta's famous Voltaic pile, invented in 1800, was long believed to be the first electric battery. In 1936, however, workers excavating a small village outside the modern-day city of Baghdad, Iraq, found something that changed how the world thought about electricity and human history. They unearthed a small copper vase plugged at both ends by an asphalt-like substance. Archaeologists opened the vase and found an iron rod inside that showed evidence of being corroded with acid. When scientists built a replica of the vase and experimented with it, they discovered that the device conducted an electric charge of 0.87 modern-day volts, roughly half the power needed by a modern wristwatch. The copper pot was actually a very ancient battery.

The electricity-conducting artifact, now known as the Baghdad battery, dates back to about 248 B.C. Scientists believe it was used for electroplating, or the process of using an electric current to transfer a thin layer of metal onto another object. Interestingly, archaeologists have found artifacts from as long ago as 2500 B.C. that seem to have been electroplated. Ancient cultures may have developed primitive battery technology for electroplating thousands of years before Volta invented his Voltaic pile.

still the basic idea behind nearly all modern batteries. "With Volta's battery, the electricity remained," says electrical engineer and microchip designer Hans Camenzind. "It could be used many times, yet the electric 'tension,' as Volta called it (and for which we now use the term voltage in his honor) would remain strong…what Volta had in fact pried out of nature was not so much the electric battery as the far more important electric current."[1]

Once Volta had set forth the basic principles of generating electrical energy using batteries, other scientists began experimenting with new metals and different kinds of acidic

substances to improve on the idea. In 1859, a French physicist named Gaston Planté experimented with a metal called lead and created the first lead acid storage battery. Like Volta's batteries, Planté's used a liquid electrolyte and was therefore very heavy and difficult to move. As the years passed, however, scientists continued to create new and better batteries, seeking models that had faster reactions and were more powerful and efficient. These batteries showed promise of being able to power objects such as vehicles. In the form of the mid-nineteenth-century battery, the dream of controlling electricity as a useful and portable source of energy had come true.

A print shows Alessandro Volta demonstrating his Voltaic pile battery to French leader Napoleon Bonaparte in 1801.

Battery Life

The development of various types of batteries was fascinating to scientists, but to the general population, the first batteries seemed like awkward, useless inventions. The battery and its electrical charge had to actually do something people would recognize as helpful. Electrical energy, or energy created by the flow of an electric charge, could be stored in a battery. However, that energy was of little use unless it could be shifted into mechanical energy, or energy that could make a tool or other mechanical object move. This was accomplished with the development of the first electric motors, devices made by hooking batteries up to moving parts to convert electrical energy into mechanical motion. When connected to an electric power source (a battery), a motor would spin. Adding an axle—a pole coming out from the middle of the motor and spinning as the motor spun—meant that an electric motor could be hooked up to other spinning elements, such as wheels, in order to make a larger object move without any effort by a human or animal.

THE ELECTRIC MOTOR

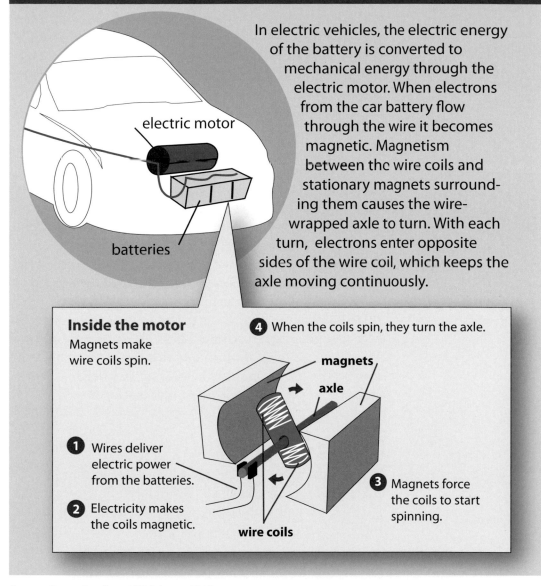

electric motor

batteries

In electric vehicles, the electric energy of the battery is converted to mechanical energy through the electric motor. When electrons from the car battery flow through the wire it becomes magnetic. Magnetism between the wire coils and stationary magnets surrounding them causes the wire-wrapped axle to turn. With each turn, electrons enter opposite sides of the wire coil, which keeps the axle moving continuously.

Inside the motor
Magnets make wire coils spin.

4 When the coils spin, they turn the axle.

magnets

axle

1 Wires deliver electric power from the batteries.

2 Electricity makes the coils magnetic.

3 Magnets force the coils to start spinning.

wire coils

Source: Data taken from WR Science, 2008.

One man who envisioned the possibilities that a battery-powered, motorized vehicle could have for society was Thomas Davenport, an American blacksmith from Vermont. In the mid-1830s, he learned about electromagnets, a new invention that combined the electric energy of a battery with the behavior of magnets. Magnets are electrically charged objects whose positive and negative poles or ends cause them to either attract or repel one another in a circular motion. Davenport built his own electromagnets and experimented with them. In 1834, he developed a model of what would today be called a DC motor, the *DC* standing for *direct current*, which is an electric current received directly from a battery. Davenport fitted a small model train and some tools in his workshop with his new motor. He received a patent for his device and dreamed of a future when America's roads would be filled with battery-operated vehicles that used his invention. Batteries and parts for Davenport's motors were expensive, however, and the people he approached as he tried to sell his idea did not see the machines as practical. Davenport died in 1851 and never saw the electric-powered vehicle enjoy the level of popularity he had envisioned. Davenport's motor was decades ahead of its time, but by the end of the nineteenth century, the electric-powered motor car had begun its rise to fame and was ready to take the world by storm.

Driving Forces

In Davenport's lifetime, people who needed to travel mostly did so on foot, on horseback, or in horse-drawn carriages. This system had worked fine for centuries, but by the late 1800s, as cities grew larger and more crowded, the abundance of horses and horse-drawn carriages led to piles of manure that polluted streets. City dwellers complained about the smell, the flies, and the poor quality of life that horse pollution caused. The public was ready to consider alternatives to the horse-drawn carriage. With the promise of potential wealth, inventors became greatly interested in the idea of building and selling vehicles that replaced manpower or horsepower with electricity—vehicles that could operate solely on batteries.

The idea of horse-free travel was not entirely new. The steam engine, which used burning coal to heat water and create steam that made wheels or other mechanical parts move, powered what became a widespread form of travel by the late 1800s: the steam locomotive train. In the United States, the completion of the transcontinental railroad in 1869 had made it possible to take a train from one end of the continent to the other. People who had to travel long distances between cities frequently opted to pay for a comfortable train ride instead of bouncing along a rutted dirt road in a horse-drawn carriage for several days. However, while trains offered a transportation alternative over long distances *between* cities, they did nothing to help with the manure pollution and inconvenience of traveling shorter distances *within* cities. Many people, especially in the wealthier classes, were interested in a new form of transportation that could take them conveniently along city streets. Small vehicles designed for personal use were suddenly an idea that captivated the imaginations of inventors and businessmen, and the race was on to create a reliable form of street transportation—a horseless carriage. "People were now

A print shows a steam engine traveling through the Sierra Nevada mountains in the late 1800s. Steam-powered trains enabled people at that time to travel long distances with relative speed and ease compared to horse-drawn carriages.

beginning to see how the horse-less carriage could benefit them," says historian Michael Dooley. "These early pioneers revolutionized the way people lived and worked. America would never be the same."[2]

Competition Among Cars

Electricity was the driving force behind what may have been the first true street-sized vehicle. Created by an English inventor named Thomas Parker in 1884, this cart-shaped contraption lacked a roof, had wooden wheels with wooden spokes, and worked very much like its horse-drawn counterparts, with one important difference: It was powered with electricity in the form of a battery. The cart's speed and steering could be regulated by its driver. People in England and the United States instantly took to the idea of personal-sized vehicles that did not need to be towed by a horse. Suddenly, new automotive possibilities were captivating the interest of inventors and buyers on both sides of the Atlantic Ocean.

Battery-operated electric motors were not the only type of motor being tinkered with. A smaller version of the steam engines that had powered trains for decades was created to fit a personal-sized passenger car that could be used within towns and cities. In 1885, a third kind of engine was invented: one that got its power by burning gasoline to create tiny explosions that made the vehicle's wheels turn. This contraption, called the internal combustion engine, came close on the heels of the first electric motors. American entrepreneurs were soon busy manufacturing all three kinds of vehicles— steam, electric, and internal combustion—and by 1900, they were competing heavily for American customers interested in buying their own personal cars.

By the turn of the twentieth century, the race to create the most popular kind of car in America was a dead heat. Each kind of vehicle had advantages and disadvantages. Steam engines were the least expensive option, and a steam-powered car offered speed, which was appealing to American drivers. The steam engine took a long time to fire up, however. It had to get hot enough to turn water into the steam that made the car go. It also required drivers to

The Subway Takes Charge

English inventor Thomas Parker created more than the first electric car. He also electrified the London Underground, the world's first city subway system. Under Parker's guidance, London's subway trains, formerly powered by steam engines, were electrified in 1890 through the addition of a third rail that carried an electric current to run the trains' motors. Electric trains are now standard public transportation in the world's biggest cities. The London Underground, known as the tube, moves 3.4 million people a day on its electric trains. The famous Paris Metro transports 4.5 million passengers per day. In Hong Kong, China, where 90 percent of all travel is done by mass transit, 7 million passengers ride electric trains daily. The American standard for electric transit systems is in New York City, the only U.S. metropolis where more than half of all households have no car and where 4.5 million people a day ride the electric subway. Electric mass transit systems are an efficient, convenient, and nonpolluting way to get around in a big city. These trains are the most commonly used electric vehicles in the world, thanks in part to the vision of nineteenth-century electrician Thomas Parker for clean, convenient urban transportation.

An electric commuter train waits at a station platform in Hong Kong, China.

make frequent stops to replace the water lost from the engine in the form of steam. Some customers were put off by the inconvenience these cars presented.

Internal combustion engines were pricier than steam engines, but they, too, could drive at high speeds. They could also travel long distances before the driver had to stop and refuel. A serious drawback to this engine, however, was that its combustion process caused it to belch black smoke and fumes. The cars were dirty, loud, and smelly. They also

A driver turns the crank of his car in order to start its engine. Crank starters, which were dangerous and required a good amount of strength to use, were a drawback of early automobiles.

lacked the ability to start without help from a crank starter. "The driver had to get out of the vehicle, insert a hand crank under the radiator, and pray that his arm or jaw would not be broken when the crank kicked back," says William Pelfrey, former director of executive communications for the General Motors Company. "It made great material for slapstick silent movie scenes but also detracted from the automobile's appeal to anyone who was muscularly challenged."[3] Crank starters were dangerous to more than just arms and jaws—the person operating the crank could be run over if the engine suddenly roared to life and set the car in motion before he could get out of the way. The crank starter was a significant sales hurdle for manufacturers of cars with internal combustion engines.

The third option among new automobiles was the electric vehicle, and it had strong advantages compared to the internal combustion engine's most serious drawbacks. Batteries provided power almost silently, compared to the rumble of internal combustion or the hissing and spewing of a steam engine. Electric vehicles were clean, too, emitting no smoky exhaust. They required less maintenance and mechanical know-how than their steam and combustion rivals. Best of all, an electric vehicle was fast and easy to start, making it an attractive option for many drivers, especially women who wanted their own car. Electric vehicles had drawbacks of their own, however. They were expensive, they could not travel as far between stops as cars with other kinds of engines could, and perhaps most importantly, they could not go as fast.

Despite their respective drawbacks, all three kinds of cars appealed to different people who could afford a new automobile. Some consumers preferred the speed and power of the internal combustion engine and were willing to put up with the smell and the dirt. Others opted for the less expensive but still speedy steam engine. And many chose the clean, quiet convenience of the electric car, often considered the most practical choice, especially in bigger cities where noise and stench drew dirty looks from passersby and where more people could afford the pricier electric car. "At the turn of the 20th century," say automobile historians Curtis Darrell Anderson and Judy Anderson, "the marketplace was equally divided with no clear indication of which type would dominate."[4] The battle among car manufacturers to create the most popular kind of car in America raged on.

Combustion Takes the Lead

By the 1920s, personal automobiles were becoming so popular that they began to change the structure of American cities and towns and the habits of Americans themselves. As more people purchased vehicles, cities began to improve their roads, covering them with a tarry substance called asphalt to make them smoother and more pleasant for drivers who had to bounce along on the slender wheels of their cars. To pay for better roads, towns and cities charged car-owning residents a fee to register their automobiles. "All autos were assessed equally in the early decades," say Anderson and Anderson, "but by the 1920s the criterion for fees had changed. A vehicle's weight became a factor. Electrics, because of the extra weight from their onboard batteries, were charged a higher fee to cover wear and tear on the road's surface."[5] Not only were electric cars more expensive to purchase in the first place, drivers also paid more to register and drive them. This became a significant drawback for the electric car.

Another blow to the electric car's reputation was its limited traveling distance and speed. New roads were being built all around the United States, and by 1914, it was possible to drive a car from one end of the country to the other using the Lincoln Highway. People no longer wanted cars just to run errands in cities. They wanted to take part in the latest American pastime—touring the country by car. Frequent stops during such a car journey were not unusual. Steam-powered cars required stops for more water; drivers of electric cars had to stop at recharging stations or pay to exchange a depleted battery with a fresh one; and internal combustion vehicles needed to be refueled with gasoline. After vast amounts of oil were discovered in the early 1900s in Texas and the northeastern United States, the gasoline that came from oil became overly abundant. Refueling stations sprang up to service every town. Gasoline could be purchased almost anywhere a touring motorist wanted to go. There were not nearly as many charging stations for electric vehicles as there were gas stations for internal combustion engines. In fact, along the new Lincoln Highway, there were no battery charging stations at all between Salt Lake City, Utah, and Sacramento, California. The electric car would run out of charge long before it had covered that distance, so it became impossible to tour the entire country in a battery-operated vehicle. Electric cars could no longer compete with engines powered by steam or internal combustion, at least among Americans who wanted to travel across the country. The popularity of the electric vehicle began to decline.

Adding to the electric car's growing number of disadvantages, in 1908 an American entrepreneur named Henry Ford

Henry Ford poses with a Model T, the first automobile to be mass produced in the United States.

chose the internal combustion engine to power his Model T, the first vehicle to be produced in large numbers. Ford wanted Model Ts to rule America's roadways. He produced thousands of the cars, which he could sell for about $600 apiece—much less money than other cars cost. It was Ford's goal for every American to be able to buy a car and go touring. The Model T, with its internal combustion engine, was affordable and readily available, and so was the gasoline to operate it. Steam-powered engines and electric vehicles began to fall further behind as Model Ts took over the nation's roadways.

The factor that finally pushed the battery-operated vehicle almost entirely out of the picture was, ironically, the incorporation of batteries in gasoline-powered vehicles. People had grown used to the noise, exhaust, and bad smell of the internal combustion engine. The one remaining drawback to this kind of car was the inconvenient hand crank needed to start it. An electric vehicle's engine, on the other hand, started up immediately from inside the car. In 1912, an engineer named Charles Kettering came up with a solution for this one lingering problem with internal combustion engines. He invented a device called an electric ignition that used electrical energy from a battery to give the combustion engine's parts the initial movement they needed to start the combustion process. By the early 1920s, Kettering's self-starter was used for all internal combustion engines. It was incredibly easy to operate, requiring only the turn of a small key to start the engine. The last remaining inconvenience to operating an internal combustion vehicle disappeared. "It was the battery and electric starter motor combination...that put the internal combustion engine on the map," says electrical engineer Bob Brant. "It made cars easy to start and easy

Upgrade: Tesla Roadster

Electric cars have been accused of wimpy acceleration, limited driving range between charges, and even a frumpy appearance. None of these can be said about the Tesla Roadster, an all-electric sports car that goes from 0 to 60 miles (97km) per hour in just 3.7 seconds, faster than almost any gasoline-powered car in its class. Introduced in 2009, the spunky speedster can drive 245 miles (394km) between battery charges. Its 288-horsepower kick comes from a 990-pound (449kg) lithium-ion battery, the densest in the automobile industry. The hefty battery is counteracted by lightweight carbon-fiber body panels that are as strong as steel but with 30 percent less mass (space shuttles are made of the same material). The Roadster plugs into any outlet and can recharge overnight. It handles as well as any sports car but runs almost silently with no tailpipe, no emissions, and no gasoline. Touted as one of the world's most coveted sports cars, the Tesla Roadster puts electric vehicles' slowpoke reputation to rest. Its one drawback may be its price tag of $101,500—and that's *after* the $7,500 federal grant for electric vehicles. For those who love fast cars and the environment equally, however, it may be a reasonable price to pay.

to use, for anyone, anywhere."[6] Gasoline-powered cars have entirely dominated the U.S. automobile industry ever since.

Electric Vehicles Today

By the 1920s, the internal combustion engine had pushed steam-powered and electric vehicles off the road. Cars with steam engines, unable to compete with the overwhelming popularity, smaller size, and greater efficiency of their

A trolley makes its way up a street in San Francisco, California, powered by electricity from the wires hanging above it. Other types of mass transit vehicles used around the world, including subways, trains, and busses, also utilize electric power.

internal combustion rivals, became obsolete. Steam-powered cars are now antique relics and museum oddities, a closed chapter in the story of automobile history. Electric vehicles, however, have held onto an important branch of the transportation market throughout the twentieth century and into modern times. A battery-operated vehicle still has advantages over internal combustion in situations where loud noise and exhaust fumes would be unwelcome. Golf carts are a good example of electric vehicles that are put to use in places where a typical combustion engine would be unwanted; golfers seek peace, quiet, and fresh air when out on the course. Forklifts, which are also electric vehicles, are commonly used in warehouses, where a smelly, noisy internal combustion engine would pollute the indoor air and be annoyingly loud to employees and customers. Electric vehicles can also be widely found in mass transit systems around the world, including subways, trams, trolleys, and trains, for which electric power is easier, safer, more reliable, and more efficient.

The electric vehicle is far from obsolete. In recent decades, the idea of battery-powered personal cars has again begun to capture the attention of many car manufacturers and buyers. Gasoline is no longer as cheap or readily available as it was a century ago, and the exhaust produced by millions of internal combustion engines operating around the globe has had negative effects on the environment and people's quality of life. As the needs and demands of drivers and society change, electric vehicles and the possibilities they offer are once again being considered as possible future rivals to the widespread and enormously popular internal combustion engine.

CHAPTER 2

Under the Hood of a Car

S ince the invention of the first automobiles in the 1800s, a great deal has changed in the automotive world. Cars certainly do not look the same today as the earliest models did. There have been constant improvements in their features and efficiency over the years. Yet, when all the modern gadgets and coatings are stripped away, what lies beneath the hoods of today's vehicles is not all that different from what drivers would have seen a century or more ago. The basic technology behind the way modern vehicles operate has changed surprisingly little since then. Anyone interested in the workings of today's cars need only look back to the earliest models of automobiles to understand what has driven them from the first battery-operated cars to the high-tech machines that dominate the roads today.

An automobile is any self-propelled passenger vehicle used for land transportation. In order to be self-propelled, automobiles simply need a power source—something to provide energy to the car's moving parts so that its wheels can turn and it can go forward. The engine is what makes gasoline-powered vehicles possible. "The distinctive feature of our civilization today, the one that makes it different from all others, is the use of mechanical power," says engineer V. Ganesan. "The great step was taken in this direction when

A woman gasses up her car at a service station in the early 1940s. The gas-powered internal combustion engine came to dominate the automobile market.

man learned the art of energy conversion from one form to another. The machine that does this energy conversion is called an engine."[7] Today's streets and highways are hosts to sports cars, pickup trucks, minivans, motorcycles, school buses, sport utility vehicles, eighteen-wheeled tractor trailers, and more, but beneath their metal bodies and often plush interiors, the engine, a machine that converts thermal or heat energy into mechanical motion, is the heart of every one of them.

Early in the twentieth century, still faced with competition from its electric and steam-powered rivals, the gasoline-fueled internal combustion engine became the popular choice among car owners and has remained so ever since. About 99 percent of cars and trucks manufactured today use an internal combustion engine. When people think of automobiles, they automatically think of internal combustion automobiles, because that is the only kind most people have owned and driven for nearly a hundred years. As the decades pass, however, and as the oil reserves that provide gasoline for internal combustion engines are harder to come by, inventors and engineers are very interested in finding different ways to power automobiles. The internal combustion engine is the standard to which all other kinds of engines are compared. To compete, electric technology must work as well as or even better than internal combustion at powering automobiles and other everyday machines. It is important, therefore, to study how the process of internal combustion works in order to understand why it remains such a popular choice for today's vehicles.

Fueling the Fire

An internal combustion engine operates on a very basic principle: Gasoline vapors are flammable. The term *internal combustion* means, literally, igniting or burning fuel, such as gasoline, inside an enclosed space. Gasoline, by far the most common fuel used in internal combustion engines, is made by processing crude oil, or petroleum, a liquid substance made mostly of combined hydrogen and carbon. Crude oil is retrieved by drilling into underground pools of it that exist deep

An internal combustion engine is the centerpiece of vehicles and other devices powered by gasoline.

beneath the earth's surface. Other chemicals are added to crude oil to make gasoline, a liquid that evaporates (turns into a gaseous vapor) easily. When gasoline vapor comes into contact with air and this mixture in turn is exposed to a flame or a spark, the vapor-and-air mixture will ignite, or catch on fire.

When gasoline ignites within an enclosed space—such as a tank or other container—the increasing heat from the rapidly burning vapor will create intense pressure that pushes out against the walls of the container. If the container is not strong enough to withstand the pressure, the ignited gasoline will cause its container to explode. Internal combustion engines, however, work by safely generating numerous small, controlled gasoline explosions within an enclosed container. Tiny amounts of gasoline vapor inside a metal chamber are exposed to a spark, which ignites the fumes. As the heated gas expands, it releases energy, but instead of making its container burst open, the heat energy instead pushes against a moving part in the container, called a piston. This process happens over and over again as the engine runs, and the moving piston can be attached to mechanical levers that are used to turn a vehicle's wheels.

An Inside Look at Internal Combustion

A German inventor named Nikolaus Otto is credited with the invention of the first internal combustion engine in 1876. The device consisted of a single metal cylinder, the inside of which was divided into two airtight spaces. The divider between the spaces was a piston, a tight-fitting disc that moved up and down within the cylinder. The top space of the cylinder held air, and the "floor" of this air-filled space was the piston. When the piston was in its uppermost position, the floor of the cylinder's upper space was pushed up toward its ceiling. This compressed, or pushed together, the air in the top part of the cylinder.

The top part of the cylinder also had two valves at the top—flapped openings to control the movement of liquids

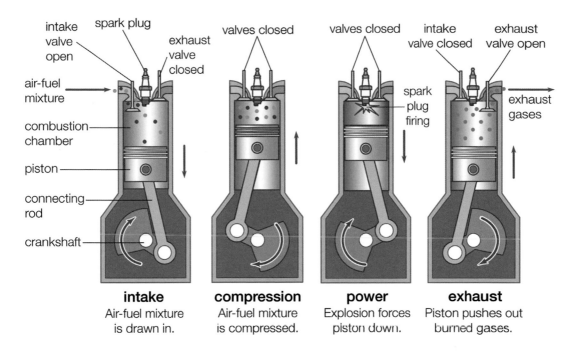

intake	compression	power	exhaust
Air-fuel mixture is drawn in.	Air-fuel mixture is compressed.	Explosion forces piston down.	Piston pushes out burned gases.

or gases. One of these valves, the inlet valve, was designed to let a small squirt of fuel, or gasoline, into the top part of the cylinder. The other valve, the exhaust valve, opened up after the fuel had been ignited to let exhaust, the chemical by-products of the explosion, out of the cylinder. The final part of Otto's setup was a spark plug, which provided the spark necessary to ignite the fuel and generate an explosion within the cylinder.

The entire device was called a four-stroke cylinder, because its piston changed position four times for every explosion of fuel. On the first stroke, the piston moved downward, pulling the "floor" of the cylinder's upper chamber down, too. This created suction in the upper part of the cylinder, and the suction pulled in a small squirt of fuel and air through the inlet valve. Then the piston, which was attached to a jointed metal arm, moved upward (its second stroke), pushing the floor of the cylinder's upper chamber toward its ceiling and compressing the fuel and air mixture into a smaller space. The spark plug then zapped, igniting the fuel and air mixture in the compressed upper chamber of the cylinder. Once ignited, the flammable fuel and air mixture greatly increased

A diagram details the four strokes of an internal combustion engine: intake, compression, power (combustion), and exhaust.

Upgrade: Gas to Diesel

In 1892, German inventor Rudolf Diesel improved on Nikolaus Otto's internal combustion engine. Diesel's engine also had an enclosed cylinder to create a small explosion and move a piston, but instead of gasoline, it used peanut oil, and instead of a spark, it used the heat of compressed air.

Tiny air molecules within a container move around freely and bump into each other. Each collision creates a small amount of heat. If the air is forced into an even smaller space, the molecules bump into each other harder and more often, increasing the temperature of the container. Oils, such as the peanut oil Diesel used, have a flash point—a temperature at which they burn spontaneously. When a squirt of oil is added to hot, highly compressed air in a cylinder, the oil ignites—no spark needed.

Diesel's first engines spit out thick, smelly exhaust and were obnoxiously loud, but they were powerful. Diesel engines are still used today in vehicles that pull heavy loads, such as tractor-

trailer rigs. Most modern diesel fuel is petroleum-based, but it can be blended with biodiesel made of vegetable or animal oils. Future diesel cars will have far better fuel economy than those that run on gasoline and may be a competitor for electric vehicles.

The first diesel engine was invented by Rudolf Diesel in 1893.

in heat, rising almost 3,632°F (2,000°C) in a mere instant. As the gas and air molecules reached this extreme temperature, they put pressure on the inner surfaces of the cylinder's compressed upper chamber. This pressure pushed against the only flexible surface of the chamber, its moving floor—the piston. As the piston was forcefully pushed down by the heat and energy of the explosion, it made the hinged arm that was attached to it revolve as well. The arm's rebounding motion sent the piston rapidly into its next stroke, forcing it back into an upward motion and compressing what was left of the burned air and gas mixture in the upper chamber of the cylinder. This forced opened the exhaust valve, which released the by-products of the ignited fuel and air mixture—the exhaust—out into the atmosphere.

Still rebounding from the hard push it received when the fuel ignited, the arm attached to the piston rotated again into a downward position, pulling the piston down with it and creating suction to draw in another squirt of fuel. The entire process was then repeated. Each explosion was powerful enough to spin the arm attached to the piston and set up the next explosion. The process was repeated continuously as long as the engine ran. The rotating arm attached to the piston in the cylinder could be connected to other turning components of an automobile, linking the energy created in the cylinder to the moving wheels. The vehicle could move forward whenever the engine was running.

A century and a half after it was invented, Otto's single-cylinder, four-stroke engine still forms the basis for the vast majority of personal automobiles on the world's roads today. A single-cylinder engine is not very powerful by modern standards, so most engines in today's vehicles have several cylinders, all working together to generate energy that is combined to give the vehicle more power. Each cylinder in a modern engine undergoes the same basic process of fuel intake, compression, combustion, and release of exhaust as Otto's first internal combustion engine did. An engine that combines the power of six or eight cylinders is powerful enough to do anything expected of a modern car, from cruising freeways to four-wheeling on a mountainside. "Cylinders have been added—two, four, six, eight, and more— and we've seen devices to limit pollution and save fuel, but the internal combustion engine is still remarkably similar to the Otto pattern of the 1870s," says American historian Tom Philbin. People today, especially in the United States, have a long-standing loyalty to the internal combustion engine. "For good or bad," Philbin says, "it's here to stay, for at least a while."[8] In spite of its overwhelming popularity among

A model of the atom shows the cluster of protons and neutrons surrounded by orbiting electrons.

engine types, however, internal combustion engines do have an old rival that is gaining renewed attention in the world of automobile research and manufacturing—the battery.

Cars and Chemistry

Internal combustion engines and the battery-powered motors that operate electric cars work in very different ways, but both involve converting one kind of energy to another in order to do the work of making a car move. Internal combustion engines convert the heat energy of burning fuel into mechanical energy, which makes a car's parts move. A battery-powered motor, on the other hand, converts *electrical* energy into mechanical force or motion. Instead of harnessing power created by combustion, batteries use energy produced by chemistry. A battery is an enclosed device that produces an electric current from chemical reactions that take place inside it, and these reactions can be just as powerful as the explosive energy of internal combustion. The battery-powered motor is the heart of the electric car.

Chemistry, which produces a battery's power, is the science of the structure, properties, and interactions of the basic elements that make up all matter in the world, whether liquid, solid, or gas. Scientists have discovered 118 different elements, or unique substances, in our universe. Elements are all around us. The air we breathe, for example, contains oxygen and hydrogen; commonly used metals, such as iron, nickel, and lead, are also elements. Each element consists of microscopic particles called atoms, which are far too small to see with the naked eye. Atoms of any element, such as gold, are like other atoms of that same element and different from atoms of all other elements. That is what makes each element distinct and unique.

An atom of any element has three parts: protons, neutrons, and electrons. Protons are particles with a positive electrical charge, neutrons are particles with no electrical charge, and electrons are particles with a negative electrical charge. Protons and neutrons cluster together to form a mass at the center of an atom. This mass is the nucleus. Negatively charged electrons orbit outside the nucleus. Every element's atoms have a certain number of protons, neutrons, and electrons, and these different numbers give the element its own unique chemical properties. A single atom of hydrogen, for example, is small, with only one proton in its nucleus. An atom of gold is much larger, with seventy-nine protons in its nucleus. Often, atoms of an element have the same number of electrons in orbit as protons in the nucleus. The positive charge of each proton and the negative charge of each electron balance each other out, creating an electrically neutral atom, one whose positive and negative charges are equal.

An atom of a single element cannot be split into anything smaller to create a different substance. However, atoms of one element often combine with each other or with atoms of other elements to form molecules. They combine with each other because opposite charges—positive and negative— attract each other. The negatively charged electrons floating around the nucleus of one atom may be attracted to the positively charged protons in the nucleus of another atom. Atoms of certain elements, when exposed to each other, have a strong tendency to bond together and form molecules. As atoms are joined or rearranged to form new and different molecules, their negatively charged electrons sometimes escape or are drawn away to float freely. The negative charge created by many tiny, free-floating electrons results in energy. Harnessing this energy, called electrochemical energy, so that it can be used to do mechanical work is the job of batteries.

Batteries: Under the Cover

Batteries are devices that contain two different substances, usually metals, whose molecules have a strong tendency to react with one another. A battery is divided into two compartments, or cells, and each metal is placed in its own compartment. The metals are then submerged in an electrolyte, a substance (usually a liquid) that reacts with the metals, breaking apart their molecules and allowing electrically charged particles to move around freely. Salt water is one common electrolyte. Sulfuric acid, used in some modern car batteries, is another. As molecules of one metal react with molecules of the electrolyte solution, the metal begins to corrode—its surface breaks apart as its molecules pull away from each other. Some negatively charged electrons escape during the rearranging of atoms and molecules, and these electrons float around in the electrolyte solution, searching for a positively charged molecule to bond with.

An electrical wire is used to connect the cell of the battery that has a high number of free-floating electrons, and thus a high negative charge, to the other cell of the battery, which holds molecules of a different metal. The other compartment has components that produce few to no free-floating electrons, and thus it has a higher overall positive charge. The negatively charged electrons in the first cell will be attracted to the positively charged molecules in the other cell and will be drawn through the wire to change locations. The

Becoming an Automotive Designer

Job Description: Automotive designers create and sketch detailed plans for the exterior and interior designs of new automobiles. They also draft and model three-dimensional automobile systems based on their knowledge of engineering principles and what consumers want in a car.

Education: Automotive designers need an undergraduate degree in automotive or industrial design. Completion of an internship in a related field may also be required by some employers.

Qualifications: This occupation requires excellent drawing and computer skills and experience with computer-aided design programs. Automotive designers need a strong background in automobile technology and manufacturing methods, vehicle safety, aerodynamics, and other features important to the design of a car. The job also requires good presentation skills and the ability to work under tight deadlines.

Additional Information: Automotive designers constantly learn about new designs, changes in customer desires, and automobile technologies. They are usually employed by design firms or automobile manufacturers.

Average Salary: $55,000 per year or higher

charged electrons have electrical energy, and as they move through the wire, their energy can be trapped. "The battery produces an external current flow from positive to negative corresponding to its internal electron flow from negative to positive,"[9] says electrical engineer Bob Brant. The energy from this electron flow can be captured and converted into mechanical energy.

Raising the Charge

Different metals and different electrolytes can be combined to create different amounts of energy. A typical Duracell or Energizer battery, for instance, contains the metals zinc and manganese in an electrolyte of alkaline (salt water). Used alone or in groups, these alkaline batteries provide enough energy to power a small device, such as a flashlight, radio, or remote-controlled car. The larger or more complicated the device, the more battery power it requires. A very large

Batteries are available in a range of sizes, depending on the amount of energy needed to power a specific device.

machine that uses a lot of power requires a large and powerful battery, usually one that uses more reactive metals than manganese and zinc. Lead is a metal commonly used in larger batteries. With sulfuric acid as an electrolyte, the lead acid battery packs a powerful punch. Electric cars of the late 1800s and early 1900s used this kind of battery, as do many contemporary electric vehicles, such as forklifts and golf carts.

A convenient feature of the lead acid battery is that it is almost fully rechargeable. Since a battery creates power by forcing molecules of a metal substance to break apart, releasing charged electrons in the process, the battery will only be able to provide electricity as long as some of the original metal remains to break down and as long as there are more free-floating negative electrons in one cell of the battery than the other. When the number of negatively charged particles in both of the battery's cells is about equal, electrons will no longer flow through the wire connecting the cells. The battery will be "dead," or no longer capable of producing power. Many batteries, including the lead acid battery, have the ability to be recharged, however. If the chemical reactions that took place can be reversed, the broken-down compounds can be reformed into the original metal. The chemical reaction process can then be started all over again.

When a rechargeable battery is connected to a power source, the electric flow pulls electrons back into the first cell of the battery. The same chemical process can be carried out and then reversed repeatedly, allowing a single battery to be used many times before it eventually wears out and needs to be replaced. Rechargeable batteries are an essential feature of modern electric vehicles, because the battery's spent energy can be easily replenished as long as the driver of the vehicle has access to an electrical outlet and time to wait for recharging.

Long Live the Battery

Batteries and automobiles have a long shared history. Every modern vehicle with an internal combustion engine has a lead acid battery onboard to give the engine its start-up

INSIDE THE LITHIUM-ION BATTERY

Lithium-ion batteries are quickly replacing lead-acid batteries as the main power source for electric vehicles. In a lithium-ion battery, sheets of a positive electrode (called a cathode) and sheets of a negative electrode (called an anode) are separated by thin sheets of plastic within an electrolyte solution. While the battery is discharging, lithium ions move from the anode to the cathode through the plastic, creating an electrical current within the electrolyte solution that can be captured and converted to mechanical energy through the car's electric motor. When a current is run through the battery during the charging process, lithium ions return to the anode.

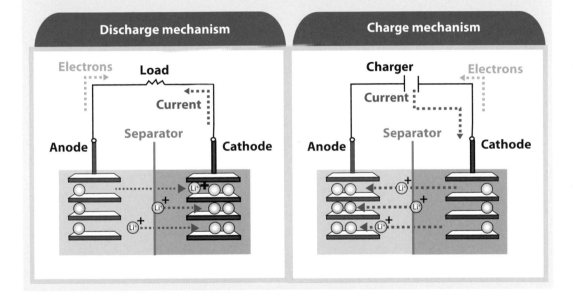

power to begin the internal combustion process. There has also been a renewed interest in creating modern vehicles that receive some or all of their power electrically from batteries. "Several major car manufacturers have designed electric cars that use various types of batteries to provide the power to drive the car," say chemists John C. Kotz, Paul Treichel, and John Raymond Townsend. However, they say, "these devices are problematic owing to their mass...in fact, the power available from any type of battery is much less than

Inside a Lithium-Ion Battery

In a lithium-ion battery, positively charged particles of the metal lithium are drawn toward carbon molecules that have a negative charge. The battery consists of thin metallic sheets of lithium cobalt oxide ($LiCoO_2$) alternated with thin sheets of carbon. These sheets are separated by a sheet of very thin, microperforated plastic that keeps the carbon and $LiCoO_2$ sheets from touching but lets tiny, electrically charged particles, or ions, pass through. The layers of metal, plastic, and carbon are placed in ether, a liquid electrolyte that helps ions move from one sheet to the other. When the battery is at full power, the positively charged lithium ions have been drawn to the sheets of carbon. As the battery discharges, the ions are drawn back through the perforated plastic to combine with the $LiCoO_2$. Once all the ions have moved to the $LiCoO_2$, an electric current is run through the battery to pull the ions back to the carbon. A lithium-ion battery can be used and recharged hundreds of times, and it packs more than twice the punch of a same-sized alkaline battery. Lithium-ion batteries are a high-tech power source for an electric car.

that available from an equivalent mass of gasoline."[10] A lead acid battery small enough to fit into a modern golf cart, for example, will stop generating power and will need to be recharged after only 12 to 18 miles (19 to 29km) of driving. A gasoline-powered golf cart, by comparison, can drive about 250 to 300 miles (402 to 483km) on a full tank of gas. Lead acid batteries are convenient for some kinds of small vehicles, but they are not an option for drivers of larger cars who have a long commute to school or work or who want to take a vacation by car.

Automobiles powered by lead acid batteries, therefore, are widely considered impractical for the needs of many of today's drivers. In the late 1980s, though, a new kind of battery called the nickel metal hydride battery became a more promising option for battery-powered vehicles. A battery of this type contains and releases a lot of energy for its size, making it a good alternative to the cumbersome lead acid battery. In the 1990s, battery technology was improved again with the lithium-ion battery, a powerful, lightweight device that is easy to recharge. Lithium-ion batteries have another perk—they lose almost none of their energy just by sitting idle, unlike most other batteries that slowly discharge even when not in use. Lithium-ion batteries are already used widely in modern gadgets like laptop computers and cell phones, but they have also been put to use as a power source for electric vehicles. With the advent of new battery options like the nickel metal hydride and the lithium-ion battery, updated electric vehicles are coming on the market, and for the first time in more than a century, drivers are starting to take this technology seriously.

CHAPTER 3

The Hybrid and the Electric Revolution

Despite the overwhelming popularity of the internal combustion engine, many of an electric car's features seem like logical advantages over its combustion-powered rivals. Battery-powered engines require no refueling at smelly gas stations, for example. The structure of electric cars is simpler, too—they basically need only a battery and a motor to turn the car's wheels—compared to the complicated mechanical operation of an internal combustion engine, with its battery, spark plugs, fuel lines, oil compartments, and dozens of other parts that all have to work together seamlessly in order for the engine to run. An electric car requires little to no maintenance, except for regular recharges and an occasional tune-up. An internal combustion vehicle, however, requires frequent maintenance, oil changes, and repair or replacement of parts that wear out after enduring so many miniature explosions. Electric cars also operate almost silently compared to the clatter and rumble of their combustion counterparts, and they emit no smelly, polluting fumes. Various models of electric cars have remained in circulation since the early twentieth century, seemingly waiting for people to choose a cleaner, quieter vehicle.

Despite the many appealing characteristics of electric cars, hurdling the popularity of internal combustion has always been a challenge for car manufacturers that want to produce and sell electric vehicles. The internal combustion engine is the only kind that most modern drivers, especially those in the United States, have ever known. When it comes to expensive items like automobiles, people tend to prefer products that are familiar to them rather than taking a risk on newer technology that could prove unreliable. This is one reason why the American public is unlikely to make an immediate shift to cars that operate completely on a battery. Any changes to American car-buying habits are bound to be slow and gradual. Not since their brief heyday at the start of

The Bersey taxi cab, one of several early types of electric vehicles, was driven on the streets of London, England, in the late 1890s.

Celebrity Status

The Toyota Prius has long stood as an idol among hybrid electric vehicles in the United States, in part because of its frequent appearances at televised events, such as the Academy Awards, over the past decade. Environmentally conscious movie stars make as much of a statement with their cars as their clothes at these highly publicized events. At the 2002 Oscars, actor Harrison Ford was one megastar who showed up in a Prius. Since then, many others have pulled up to red-carpet occasions in their hybrid vehicles instead of limousines or sports cars. Big-screen favorites George Clooney, Cameron Diaz, Meryl Streep, and Leonardo DiCaprio have all been seen driving around in a Prius. Actress Sandra Bullock even swapped her sporty Porsche for the more eco-friendly Toyota hybrid. As a small but notable token to the hybrid wave of fame in modern America, a 2006 version of the board game Monopoly traded the classic Packard Roadster playing piece for a miniature Toyota Prius, a symbol of changing times and changing driving habits in America.

George Clooney waves at the Academy Awards after arriving in a Toyota Prius. Several celebrities have brought attention to the Prius and other electric cars by driving them to public appearances or as their own personal vehicles.

the twentieth century have electric cars been seen on public streets in large numbers. To help ease the tough transition from internal combustion to electric vehicles, a few automobile manufacturers have started experimenting with cars that blend both types of engines. These semi-electric cars are called hybrids.

Marrying Technologies Together

A hybrid vehicle is one that uses two or more sources of power, such as electricity and gasoline, to create the mechanical energy the vehicle needs for motion. "Hybrid vehicles

THE STANDARD HYBRID AND THE PLUG-IN HYBRID

All gasoline-electric hybrids run on an electric battery and a gasoline-powered engine, but new models hope to boost mileage and lessen trips to the gas station by adding a plug-in option.

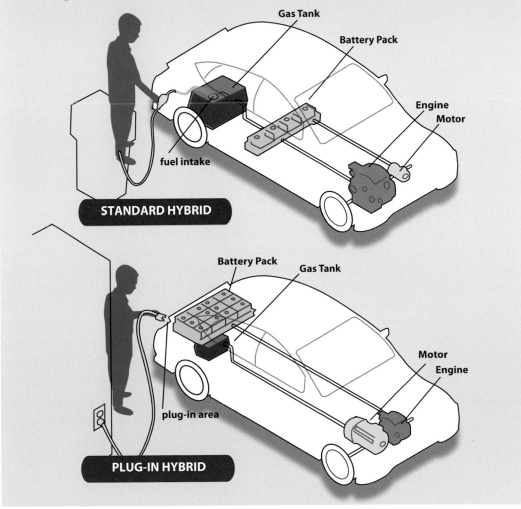

Gas Tank

Battery Pack

Engine
Motor

fuel intake

STANDARD HYBRID

Battery Pack   Gas Tank

Motor
Engine

plug-in area

PLUG-IN HYBRID

appear to offer an interim solution" for the problem of gasoline's disadvantages and electric cars' unpopular image and features, say chemists John C. Kotz, Paul Treichel, and John Raymond Townsend. "[Hybrid] vehicles combine a small gasoline-fueled engine with an electric motor and batteries for storage of electric energy."[11] The engine and motor often share duties—the internal combustion engine can provide the burst of power needed to get the car moving, but once it is cruising, the battery-powered electric motor may take over to keep the wheels turning. Many hybrid cars also include built-in battery chargers: The brake system of the car captures heat energy that would otherwise be lost during the braking process. This energy is sent back to the battery to recharge it, and the battery can store any extra energy for future use. Called regenerative braking, this battery-recharging braking system also reduces wear and tear on an electric vehicle's brakes, so they require maintenance less often.

Hybrid cars may be an important technological step between automobiles that run solely on combustible fuel and cars that are entirely battery powered. "The motor industry generally regards hybrid vehicles as a short to medium term measure before long range electric cars…are the norm," says electric vehicle retailer and enthusiast Michael Boxwell. "A hybrid car provides significantly improved economy, as the electric motor takes away much of the stress from the internal combustion engine."[12] By blending some of the features people like most about an internal combustion engine with the advantages of an electric car, hybrids are becoming much more popular among car buyers and are seen more frequently in automobile dealerships and on the world's roads with each passing year.

Hybrids Hit the Road

Probably the best-known modern hybrid and the one that has gained the most attention in the United States in the past decade is the Toyota Prius. Touted as being able to drive 50 miles (80km) on a single gallon of gas, compared to the average 34 miles (55km) per gallon Americans can expect from most internal combustion cars of the same size, the Prius has become a symbol of more efficient, responsible,

SALES OF THE TOYOTA PRIUS

The Toyota Prius, currently in its 3rd generation, is an example of a successful gasoline-electric hybrid in the general automobile market. In the fall of 2010, the Toyota Motor Company announced that over 2 million Prius hybrids had been sold worldwide.

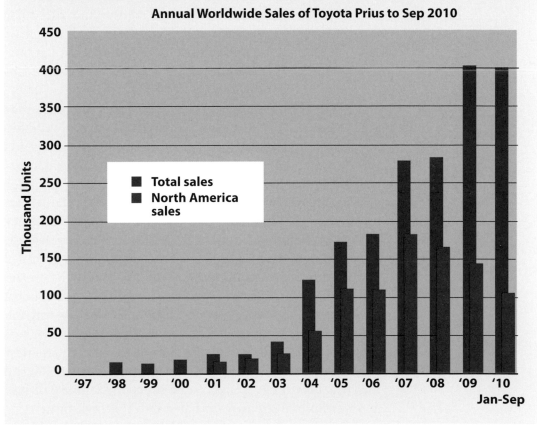

Annual Worldwide Sales of Toyota Prius to Sep 2010

Source: Data taken from "Worldwide Prius Cumulative Sales Top 2M Mark; Toyota Reportedly Plans Two New Prii Variants for the US By End of 2012." Green Car Congress. October 7, 2010. www.greencarcongress.com/2010/10/worldwide-prius-cumulative sales-top-2m-mark-toyota-reportedly-plans-two-new-prius-variants-for-the-.html#tp.

and environmentally friendly driving. Equipped with a four-cylinder gasoline engine paired with a 200-volt electric motor that recharges continuously whenever the car brakes and that can also be plugged into an electrical outlet, the Prius has won many awards for its efficiency, minimal pollution rate, and low cost of operation. It first appeared on the American market in 2000 and was named North American Car of the Year in 2004 (an award voted on by automotive journalists). The modern Prius is a roomy, mid-sized family car packed with technically advanced features. It even comes with an optional sunroof that uses solar power to ventilate the car so the interior temperature does not become uncomfortable even if the Prius is parked in the sun on a hot day.

The successful sales record of the Prius proved to car manufacturers that buyers were interested in hybrid vehicles. Many more automobile companies now offer hybrid designs as well. One popular model is the Ford Escape Hybrid, powered by a nickel-metal hydride battery and a four-cylinder gasoline engine. When driven at moderate speeds, the car can travel 41 miles (66km) per gallon of gas and can go 700 miles (1,127km) before needing to be refueled. It runs solely on battery power when coasting at speeds less than 47 miles (76km) per hour, using its gasoline engine only when the car needs to drive faster or accelerate quickly. The Honda Civic Hybrid is another popular car model, also boasting the ability to drive an average of 41 miles (66km) per gallon of gasoline. The Civic Hybrid was named one of the "Greenest Vehicles of 2010" by the American Council for an Energy Efficient Economy (ACEEE) due to its efficient use of fuel and its minimal release of exhaust into the environment.

Hybrid cars like these help address many of the problems seen in internal combustion engines, such as exhaust pollution and the use of large amounts of gasoline. Hybrids also steer around common complaints about all-electric cars. They can drive at least as far as a vehicle with an internal combustion engine before needing to be refueled, and they can combine their electric motor and gasoline engine to give the car the same power and speed that internal combustion engines are known for. Most modern hybrids also do not require their owners to plug them into a wall outlet after every single use the way some electric cars do. Hybrids have many advantages over both their electric and their internal combustion relatives, making them an increasingly popular choice for drivers. According to the *Wall Street Journal*, the Toyota Prius and the Ford Fusion were among the top twenty cars in the United States in 2010 in terms of total sales.

The Downside of Hybrids

Despite their growing popularity, hybrids have drawbacks. Most are small to mid-sized cars, seating four to five passengers with limited cargo space. They are efficient for running errands around town or commuting to work, but they do not meet the high demand in the United States for large vehicles capable of carrying more than five people, transporting large loads of cargo, driving off-road, towing a trailer, or handling well in bad weather. The most popular category of car in the United States today is the full-sized variety, a class of car that consists of sport utility vehicles (SUVs), minivans, and pickup trucks. According to the *Wall Street Journal*, about fifty thousand more full-sized vehicles than cars were bought in the United States in 2010. Mid-sized hybrids are at a disadvantage as long as Americans prefer bigger vehicles.

Full-sized vehicles do have several perks that smaller cars (and many hybrids) lack. One of these perks is four-wheel drive. This is the ability of the engine to give the right

Automobile manufacturers have created hybrid versions of full-size vehicles such as the Chevrolet Silverado to match consumer preferences for trucks, minivans, and sport utility vehicles (SUVs).

amount of power to each of a vehicle's wheels to keep it from skidding or slipping on different kinds of surfaces. This ability is necessary for maneuvering a vehicle in slick or unstable terrain like a snowy street or rugged dirt road. Many full-sized vehicles also have the power to tow accessories like a camper, a boat, or a pair of jet skis. Electric cars and even hybrids have traditionally been unable to provide enough horsepower (a standard measure of the maximum power of a vehicle's engine) and torque (the amount of force in a rotational motion, such as turning a wheel) to carry out these tasks. As long as the powerful internal combustion engine can do more of the things that Americans want in a vehicle, it will continue to trounce even the hybrid in popularity, much less any vehicle that runs on electricity alone, however "green" (environmentally friendly) it may be. "There is not a groundswell toward green vehicles in the United States," says Bob Lutz, Vice Chairman of the General Motors Company.

Inside Regenerative Braking Systems

A traditional automobile braking system is a set of pads that apply friction, or pressure, to the car's wheels to make them stop turning. Most modern hybrids and electric cars use a regenerative braking system instead. An electric car motor pulls energy from the battery in the form of electricity and converts it into mechanical energy, which is used to make the car's wheels turn in a forward motion. In a car with a regenerative braking system, the motor works the opposite way when the driver presses the brake pedal. Instead of pushing the car's wheels forward as it does while driving, the motor exerts energy when braking to turn the wheels the other direction, creating tension that slows the wheels' forward movement. Meanwhile, it retrieves energy from the heat generated by stopping the wheels. The motor converts this heat energy to electrical energy and sends it back to the battery. Every time the car slows down, the battery gets a bit of energy in return. Regenerative braking systems do not stop a car as quickly as friction brakes, so many electric and hybrid cars have backup friction-braking systems for emergencies. Drivers of cars with regenerative brakes can be thankful for red lights and traffic jams—they help recharge the battery.

"In fact," he says, "they're a very hard sell,"[13] because buyers still prefer bigger, powerful vehicles.

In response to such complaints, automakers have begun to offer more powerful vehicles in a hybrid form. Chevrolet, for example, a General Motors manufacturer, now produces hybrid versions of its popular SUV, the Tahoe, as well as its Silverado pickup truck. According to Chevrolet, these vehicles "just happen to have the same city fuel economy as a [Volkswagen] Beetle"[14] but are also equipped with powerful internal combustion engines. They have the ability to shift to internal combustion in situations that call for more power. Although their efficiency is still about 20 miles per gallon, much less than that of hybrids like the Toyota Prius, these hybrid pickups and SUVs use less fuel than their non-hybrid counterparts. "Ultimately by 2020 we figure that 80 percent of vehicles will require some sort of hybridization,"[15] Lutz says, if automakers are to meet rising expectations among consumers for better fuel economy and less pollution from their vehicles. Unfortunately, hybrid vehicles also cost more money to buy, in part because their huge batteries are expensive and also because new technology is always pricey to develop. A hybrid version of a car or truck is usually harder to find and costs at least $3,000 more, on average, than the more commonly produced internal combustion version of the same vehicle. Many consumers are unwilling to pay more money up front to purchase a car, even if it costs them less to operate and maintain it in the long run.

Yet another complaint against hybrid vehicles is that they are still not "green" enough. They continue to use gasoline (some models, such as the Chevrolet Silverado hybrid, run entirely on gasoline much of the time, in spite of being hybrids), and therefore they still emit exhaust pollution into the environment. People are interested in completely electric cars that use *no* gasoline and emit *no* damaging exhaust fumes into the environment. To compete in the American automobile market, such a car would have to run on battery power entirely but still travel as fast and as far as hybrids and internal combustion engines before it needed to be recharged. Purely electric vehicles have thus been confined to mostly non-highway uses, such as navigating golf courses.

Automotive inventors are now on a quest, however, to create an electric car that operates on battery power alone but works just as well as any internal combustion engine, one that can capture the hearts of an American public that has so long been loyal to internal combustion. Engineers and technicians working for the Chevrolet and Nissan companies finally have seemed to crack the tough electric-automobile market with the Chevrolet Volt and the Nissan LEAF, two vehicles that could start to change the way Americans think about driving.

All Charged Up

The Chevrolet Volt, introduced in late 2010, is a sleek-looking passenger car that can drive around town on battery power alone but has enough speed and power to keep up with hybrids and internal combustion engines. A huge, rechargeable lithium-ion battery powers the Volt. With a length of 5.5 feet (1.7m) and a weight of 380 pounds (172kg), the T-shaped battery runs almost the whole length of the car, providing the Volt with enough horsepower to accelerate from 0 to 60 miles (97km) per hour in eight seconds and to cruise at 100 miles (161km) per hour. The quiet, battery-powered engine releases no exhaust to the environment. The car also uses a regenerative braking system to help recharge the battery while driving. To increase its efficiency even more, the Volt's body is extremely aerodynamic, allowing air to flow smoothly over, under, and around the car it as it drives. This reduces wind resistance, or air's tendency to push back against the car as it moves at a high rate of speed.

The Volt can be plugged into any wall outlet to recharge. It takes about ten hours to completely recharge the battery when using a 120-volt outlet, the kind used for any household appliance like a toaster or hair dryer. If the Volt's owner installs a more powerful, 240-volt charging station, the Volt recharges in just four hours. The car can drive 35 miles (56km) on a fully charged battery. "Over two thirds of Americans commute 35 miles or less per day," says Pamela Fletcher, one of the chief engineers who designed the Chevy

Volt, "so most people will be able to have all-electric transportation most of the time."[16]

The Volt's 35-mile range is impressive for an electric car that accelerates and can easily cruise at freeway speeds. The Volt may easily cover the distance that most Americans *have* to drive each day. Nevertheless, it still cannot compare to the much farther distances that an internal combustion engine can travel before needing to be refueled. The Volt's designers therefore made a compromise, adding a small internal combustion engine whose only job is to power a generator, a device that converts mechanical energy to electrical energy. The gasoline-powered generator can be used to recharge the Volt's battery if power gets low. Using this system, the Volt can drive 340 additional miles (547km) before needing to be plugged in or refueled at a gas station to keep running the generator. At a cost of $41,000, the innovative Volt is a hybrid when it needs to be, but for everyday driving, it is often possible for Volt owners to avoid buying and burning any gasoline at all, something no other modern hybrid

An owner of a Chevy Volt shows his car plugged into a 240-volt charging station installed in his garage.

has yet been able to promise. "In over 100 years," says Fletcher, "the combustion engine has been the primary source of propulsion. Now we have choices."[17]

Branching Away from Hybrids

Unlike the Volt, the Nissan LEAF, also introduced in late 2010, is a purely electric car—it has no gasoline-powered parts onboard and therefore no tailpipe. It puts no pollution into the environment at all. The LEAF uses lithium-ion batteries—a hefty pack of forty-eight battery modules sits beneath the floorboards of the car, giving it a low center of gravity that allows it to make sharp, smooth turns. Like the Volt, the LEAF uses a regenerative braking system that helps to recharge the batteries whenever the car is slowing down. A main difference between the LEAF and the Volt, however, is that in a LEAF, when the battery power is low, the driver must stop and recharge the battery to avoid being stranded. There is no secondary power source to keep the car running. Also unlike the Volt, the LEAF has a maximum speed of 57 miles (92km) per hour and operates best at lower speeds of about 20 to 40 miles (32 to 64km) per hour, since greater speed generates higher wind resistance that drains battery power. The LEAF's battery also drains quickly if the driver uses the car's heater or air conditioning, and driving uphill takes more battery power, too. The LEAF can drive up to 138 miles (222km) on a single charge under ideal conditions, but its range is closer to about 60 miles (97km) per charge under most driving conditions.

Customers who want to own a LEAF are required to have a 240-volt charging station installed in their garage or driveway before they can purchase the car. The cost of the charging station and its installation are added to the car's $33,000 price tag. In cities that lack roadside charging stations, a LEAF driver must pay attention to the car's dashboard, which tells how much battery power is left and how

soon the driver must return home to recharge. For some people, especially those who live in very hot or cold climates, the limited range of a Nissan LEAF makes it impractical. Nevertheless, the car's exhaust-free operation and its quiet engine, barely louder than a ceiling fan in an average home, are big selling points. For many drivers, the LEAF's battery-powered driving range is a perfect fit for their daily driving needs. "People recognize a new urban mobility, a turning point, and they want to be part of it," says Carlos Tavares, chairman of Nissan Americas. "The Nissan LEAF will fit perfectly with their daily life and driving habits."[18]

A Nissan LEAF, which is powered solely by electricity, receives a charge in a dealer showroom.

Cyclist Speaks Out

A famous spokesperson can help boost the popularity of any new product, and the LEAF, Nissan's new all-electric car, has had a healthy dose of support from seven-time Tour de France–winning cyclist Lance Armstrong. After spending much of his life pedaling the world's roadways alongside exhaust-spewing vehicles, Armstrong is an outspoken supporter of Nissan's efforts to build and market an affordable, zero-emission vehicle that has no need for an exhaust pipe. "The quality of the air is a significant issue," he says in an interview at Nissan's U.S.A. website. "We've got to do some things differently…and the LEAF fits in there." The Nissan LEAF is one of the sponsors of Armstrong and his racing team. "It's the first of its kind," he says of the car. "I'm excited to be one of the first people to have one." As one of the world's best-known athletes, Armstrong's endorsement for the environmentally friendly LEAF may help bring even more all-electric vehicles onto the market in years to come. "I think this is really a tipping point," Armstrong says.

Quoted at the website of Nissan USA, www.nissanusa.com/leaf-electric-car/index?dcp=ppn.39666654.&dcc=0.216878497#/leaf-electric-car/video/all/LEAF_advertising/lance_armstrong_talks_leaf.

A Perfect Fit for City Drivers

The rechargeable-at-home Volt and LEAF, along with electric-car hybrids, are choices that appeal to more drivers every year, especially in cities. Vehicles like the LEAF that can run entirely on electricity over short distances are far better suited to city travel than are internal combustion engines. Cities are notorious for stop-and-go driving—traffic moves forward a short way, then the cars stop at traffic lights or stop signs before moving forward again. Even freeways, which have no traffic lights or stop signs, frequently get jammed up with traffic and become stop-and-go situations. Internal combustion engines are required to produce an extra burst of power from multiple rapid combustions in order to make a vehicle accelerate from a standstill. They also burn gasoline even while sitting motionless in traffic, because their engines are still running. Internal combustion engines use a great deal of fuel and emit a lot of exhaust in stop-and-go traffic, even if they only travel a short distance. An electric car, however, handles stop-and-go traffic very well. Its battery-powered engine uses very little energy when idling as the car sits motionless. The motor can also be turned off and on again easily without needing to restart a complicated ignition process the way an internal combustion engine does every time the engine is turned on.

The skyline of Los Angeles, California, rises from a haze of smog caused by the exhaust from internal combustion engines.

Hybrids and fully electric vehicles can be much more convenient and cost-effective than internal combustion engines for city drivers. There are other very strong reasons for cities to be looking at electric alternatives for vehicles, however, both now and in the future. In big cities like Los Angeles, California, the air is clouded with brown smog, the product of millions of internal combustion engines emitting exhaust into the air. Smog is a constant, visible reminder of the pollution that is being caused by internal combustion vehicles with every passing day, and it is one of the key issues forcing drivers, automobile manufacturers, and government officials to plan for a future in which internal combustion engines are things of the past.

CHAPTER 4

Electric Cars in the Modern World

E very internal combustion engine, even in a hybrid vehicle, uses gasoline and puts exhaust into the atmosphere. Exhaust is what comes out the tailpipe of every car with an internal combustion engine. It consists of molecules of gases left over after combustion, such as nitrogen dioxide, carbon monoxide, and carbon dioxide, the main by-products of the combustion process. People have long been aware that a dependence on internal combustion engines may not be a good thing for society in the long term, not only because of the cost and availability of gasoline but also because of pollution. Drivers have given the idea of making a shift to electric cars serious consideration at various times over the past century, especially during periods of high gasoline costs or concern about the environment. "A century ago the notion of the electric car as the 'car of tomorrow' was commonly held by some of the important people involved in automotive development," says Gijs Mom, cofounder of the International Association for the History of Transport, Traffic and Mobility. "After World War II another wave of electric enthusiasm started in the United States. It rolled over the industrialized world during the 1960s and 1970s."[19] Again in the 1990s, as air pollution and gasoline prices became an increasing concern for more Americans, there was strong interest in the idea that electric cars might replace those with combustion engines. That interest in electric vehicles continues today.

With the invention of newer, denser, and stronger power sources like the lithium-ion battery, hybrids and all-electric vehicles once more seem to be not only interesting options but also practical ones. In modern times, the pressure to start replacing internal combustion engines with electric varieties that cause no pollution and require no gasoline seems more urgent than ever. Electric cars are no longer merely a curiosity. In a changing world where laws, regulations, and politics are working against internal combustion, electric vehicles eventually may be the only kind available for people to drive in the years and decades to come.

BITS & BYTES
25%
Percentage of the world's total energy that is consumed by the United States (which has less than 5% of the world's population)

Environmental Pressures to Go Electric

Internal combustion engines are just one example of the industrial nature of human beings. Over the past several thousand years, people have vastly changed the world by building cities, flattening forests, terracing hillsides, and accomplishing many other feats to make human life more convenient. Around the year 1800, at the dawn of the Industrial Revolution, people began to invent new technologies to power factories and vehicles. They started retrieving energy-rich substances called fossil fuels, including coal and petroleum, from the earth and burning these materials to create a power source for homes, businesses, and new forms of transportation, such as the automobile. In many ways, human technology has greatly improved living standards by making electricity possible and giving people great freedom to drive almost anywhere on land they want to go, or even to fly around the world in airplanes.

Unfortunately, burning fossil fuels has caused many problems, too. The chemicals and gases released in the burning process, including carbon and nitrogen gases, have mingled with Earth's air. Fresh air is a naturally balanced mixture of oxygen and nitrogen gases required by all living things on earth. Over the past two centuries, the burning of fossil fuels has begun to alter the very air that makes life on Earth possible. In many places around the world, environmental changes are visible in a blanket of dirty brown smog, air that is filled with particles and chemicals released during the burning of fossil fuels. These particles mix with the fresh air that people and animals normally breathe. Smog is a growing concern around the world, in part because it is ugly. In Hong Kong, China, smog is so thick that the city's skyline, once one of the world's best-known and most beautiful urban views, is scarcely visible anymore. The tops of the buildings disappear into a brown cloud of polluted air. Far worse than being ugly,

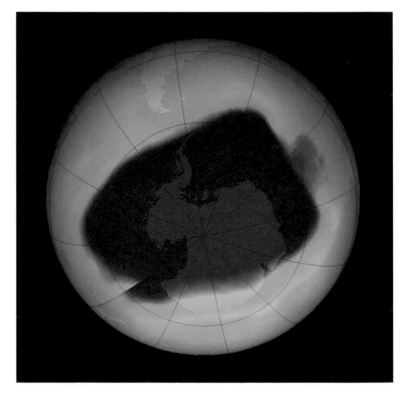

A satellite image of Earth is colorized to illustrate damage to the ozone, which has been blamed on pollution caused by the burning of fossil fuels to create electricity. Dark purple areas over Antarctica show where the ozone levels are lowest.

smog is physically harmful, too, causing breathing problems for people and animals who fill their lungs with polluted air whenever they go outside.

By-products of burnt fossil fuels not only fill breathable air with unwanted gases and particles, they also interact with ozone, oxygen gas that forms a protective layer about

Possible Blackouts

Hybrid cars like the Chevy Volt and Nissan LEAF can be plugged into a standard wall outlet at home, a convenient feature for owners. Electric companies, however, foresee problems as more of these electric cars are purchased. A hybrid car plugged into a standard 120-volt outlet uses as much energy as a small air conditioning unit. If the owner installs a 240-volt recharging station in the garage, the car will charge faster but will draw more power to do so—as much power as an average home might use in an entire day. A few Chevy Volts or Nissan LEAFs on the same street will be like adding a few extra houses, and this could overwhelm the power supply. The worry is especially great for warm cities where power outages are already common in summer, when people crank up their air conditioning. Adding electric cars to these cities' power burdens will likely require expensive changes to the

power structure, such as installing extra transformers to city blocks to prevent blackouts. Utility companies may have to pay for such improvements by charging more for power, but to drivers of plug-in cars, preserving the environment may be worth the added expense.

Ford Motor Company displays a 240-volt in-home charging station at the 2011 North American International Auto Show.

11 miles (18km) above the surface of Earth. Ozone acts like a blanket to shield Earth from the sun's harmful ultraviolet rays and keep the planet's surface a tolerable temperature for life. There is concern that chemicals released as by-products during the burning of fossil fuels have interacted with the ozone layer. Since 1985, a hole forming in the ozone layer and a gradual rise in Earth's surface temperature (a phenomenon known as global warming) have been increasingly blamed on human activities such as the burning of oil and coal in power plants to generate electricity. Global warming has been blamed on automobiles specifically, because their combustion engines release harmful chemicals and gases into the air.

There has been much debate about whether global warming is in fact caused or worsened by millions of people driving cars with combustion engines. Smog and air pollution, however, are visible and undeniable proof that in most big cities around the world, where streets are crowded with vehicles, internal combustion engines and the gases they release are doing more harm to the environment with every passing year. "The transportation sector is the second largest source of CO_2 emissions in the U.S.," says the U.S. Environmental Protection Agency. "Automobiles and light-duty trucks account for almost two-thirds of emissions from the transportation sector and emissions have steadily grown since 1990."[20] There is growing pressure not only in the United States but around the world to scale back the exhaust that comes from combustion engines and contributes to air pollution. The idea of replacing combustion engines with electric vehicles that release no emissions into the environment is rapidly gaining in popularity as a result.

Finding Fault with Fossil Fuels

Pollution is not the only strike against the internal combustion engine. Vehicles depend on gasoline to operate, and gasoline is made from crude oil, a liquid substance pumped from deep below Earth's surface. Crude oil, also known as petroleum, is a fossil fuel—it is formed from the decomposed, fossilized bodies of tiny plants and animals that lived

OW COAL WAS FORMED

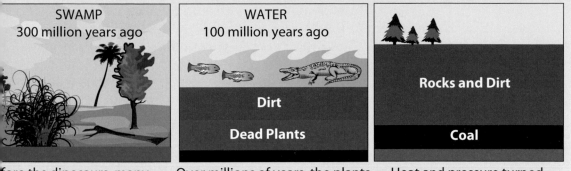

SWAMP 300 million years ago	WATER 100 million years ago	
	Dirt	Rocks and Dirt
	Dead Plants	Coal

fore the dinosaurs, many
nt plants died in swamps.

Over millions of years, the plants were buried under water and dirt.

Heat and pressure turned the dead plants into coal.

TROLEUM AND NATURAL GAS FORMATION

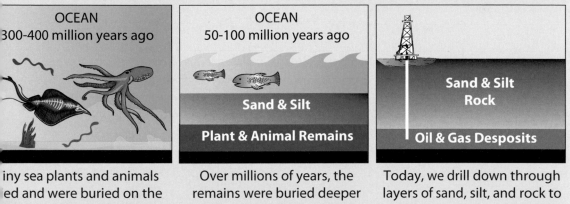

OCEAN 300-400 million years ago	OCEAN 50-100 million years ago	
	Sand & Silt	Sand & Silt Rock
	Plant & Animal Remains	Oil & Gas Desposits

iny sea plants and animals
ed and were buried on the
cean floor. Over time, they
ere covered by layers of silt
and sand.

Over millions of years, the remains were buried deeper and deeper. The enomous heat and pressure turned them into oil and gas.

Today, we drill down through layers of sand, silt, and rock to reach the rock formations that contain oil and gas deposits.

Data taken from www.eia.doe.gov/kids/energy.cfm?page=coal_home#tab2 and www.eia.doe.gov/kids/energy.cfm?page=oil_home#tab2

in prehistoric oceans millions of years ago. All that remains of those ancient living things today are pools of petroleum, a substance made mostly of the elements hydrogen and carbon. Hydrogen-carbon molecules are useful because they store a great deal of energy that is released when they are broken apart, such as when they are burned. Crude oil is the main ingredient in gasoline, and it must be pumped from beneath the ground in one of the places where stores of it exist.

Fossil fuels do not exist everywhere—most areas where they can be found were once ancient seabeds, and the main stores of the world's fossil fuels are in the Middle East, in countries such as Saudi Arabia and Iraq. This forces nations like the United States, which uses a huge amount of crude oil, to depend on smaller countries that supply it. Political

From Drilling to Mining

Fossil fuels like crude oil and coal have dominated the energy production market for the past hundred years, but the next century is shaping up to be the rare-metals era. Lithium is one metal that has been in high demand around the world ever since the lithium-ion battery became a feature of technological gadgets from laptops to cell phones. Now that electric cars are being manufactured with massive lithium-ion batteries, the world's demand for this metal is rising steeply. Currently, China produces 95 percent of the world's rare earth elements, including lithium. If countries like the United States shift from fossil fuels to battery technology for powering vehicles, they could become as dependent on China's metals as they are on the Middle East's crude oil. The good news is that although China produces far more rare metals than any other country,

it contains only about 36 percent of the world's total reserves of rare elements. The United States itself has rare metals in abundance. If Americans can find stores of metals like lithium and develop an affordable way to mine and produce them, the country and its future battery-operated vehicle industry could become far more self-sufficient than it has ever been while depending on crude oil.

Lithium is a soft alkali metal that is mined for use in various types of batteries.

relationships with these countries can be tense. They hold a lot of power over larger nations—if they were to refuse to drill for oil and sell it, the result would be disastrous, since so many countries depend on fossil fuels for their very way of life. "Dependence on imported oil is especially significant for the industrialized democracies of the free world," say political scientists Clarke E. Cochran, Lawrence C. Mayer, T. R. Carr, and N. Joseph Cayer. "The West's economic stability depends upon the uninterrupted flow of oil from the Islamic world and, therefore, upon political stability in the Middle East."[21] Americans who rely daily on their cars ultimately depend on the Middle East to provide gasoline. Many Americans are growing wary of the link between our internal combustion engines and the activities of Middle Eastern nations, many of which experience domestic unrest and may be home to terrorist groups that are hostile to the United States.

Not only is it a problem that fossil fuels come from politically unstable places, but the supply is also limited. Petroleum is burned and used up quickly in a car's engine. That same petroleum, however, was millions of years in the making. Once Earth's current stores of fossil fuels have been pumped dry, it will be millions of years until there could be more. Fossil fuels are a nonrenewable resource, meaning they cannot be regrown or replaced at the same rate people are using them. Humans around the world are depleting petroleum at an alarming rate, burning 25 billion barrels of it every year—and supplies are running out. Scientists predict that if people continue using fossil fuels at the rate they currently do, the supply of these fuels will dwindle by the year 2050 or sooner. It may not be the end of gasoline entirely at that point, but it certainly will be the end of *affordable* gasoline. Refueling a car that uses an internal combustion engine will become too expensive for an average driver.

In the past decade alone, the cost of gasoline in the United States has sometimes risen to more than $4 per gallon, a price that has forced people to drive less, walk more, and even buy cars such as hybrids that use less gasoline. Scientists and economists warn that gasoline prices will only rise higher as fossil fuels become more scarce. "One day we will run out of oil," says Dr. Fatih Birol, chief economist at the International Energy Agency (IEA) in Paris. "We have to leave oil before oil leaves us, and we have to prepare ourselves for that day…The earlier we start, the better, because all of our economic and social system is based on oil, so to change from that will take a lot of time and a lot of money and we should take this issue very seriously."[22] Freedom from high-priced gasoline is one of the main reasons why more people are becoming interested in electric cars. Many national and local governments want laws that encourage scientists to invent such cars and that persuade citizens to drive them.

City Life and the Electric Car

In many countries around the world, electric vehicles are easily gaining in popularity, and not only because they pollute less and require no gasoline. They also seem to better fit the lifestyle of people living in certain cities. London, for example, is a huge city with crowded streets and limited parking, and a small electric car is easier to maneuver and easier to park in tight spaces. The city offers other incentives to drivers of electric cars, too—it waives many parking and driving fees that owners of gasoline-powered cars must pay, and it has installed about 250 charging stations for plug-in vehicles, making it convenient for drivers to recharge wherever they go.

In the United States, however, even with gas prices rising and pollution clouding the skies, people are far more reluctant to give up on internal combustion engines. Modern U.S. society, after all, has been built around the idea that most citizens drive gasoline-powered cars. Entire towns and cities have been built in the past hundred years with vehicles in mind. Parking lots and parking garages provide oversized spaces for oversized cars—and plenty of them—and drivers prefer the convenience of being able to park their cars as close as possible to their destination. Roads are dotted with gas stations so that drivers are never stranded by an empty tank. Americans can go almost anywhere in the nation in a gasoline-fueled car. Refueling is always fast and easy.

Electric cars, on the other hand, have different needs. Unlike gas stations, there is not a recharging center on every

street corner for drivers' convenience, and long drives spanning a few hundred miles between cities would be impossible to complete on one charge of an electric car's battery. Even if there were battery charging stations along the way, batteries big enough to power a car take hours to recharge, compared to the mere minutes it takes to refill a gas tank. A shift to electric cars would require American drivers to change many of their habits and expectations for driving. It would also require most people to trade in a functional vehicle that has a combustion engine in order to purchase a new electric car, most of which are expensive because of the high cost of making large batteries. The higher price tag of electric cars, paired with the fact that recharging takes time, has made them an unpopular option in the United States. Hybrid vehicles that blend battery power and combustion are a promising middle step, but a complete abandonment of gasoline-fueled vehicles is not likely to happen anytime soon by Americans' choice alone. "Even if the nation moves toward plug-in hybrid-electric vehicles and expected improvements in battery technology are made, there will

Drivers of electric cars in London, England, can use public charging stations to power their vehicles, one of several incentives that city offers to encourage the use of electric vehicles.

be a substantial market for liquid fuels for some time,"[23] say former Central Intelligence Agency director Jim Woolsey and electric vehicle pioneer Chelsea Sexton.

In response to this unwillingness to abandon internal combustion, American lawmakers have begun to experiment with different ways to encourage the public, especially in big cities, to consider driving electric cars or hybrid vehicles. In 1990, the federal government passed the Clean Air Act, which limits the amount of carbon dioxide emissions a vehicle can produce. In California, which controls production of 10 percent of the nation's vehicles and where air pollution in cities like Los Angeles and Sacramento is notoriously high, the state government has tried passing even stricter limits on vehicle emissions. As a result, automobile manufacturers that want to sell cars to California's millions of drivers must build models that produce fewer emissions. California has also experimented with programs that encourage automobile makers to produce more zero emission vehicles (ZEVs), which are purely electric cars that produce no exhaust emissions at all. "In order to meet California's health based air quality standards, greenhouse gas emission reduction goals and to reduce our dependence on foreign oil, the cars we drive and the fuel we use must be transformed away from petroleum,"[24] says California's Air Resources Board.

Simply putting more electric vehicles on the market will not guarantee that drivers will buy them, however. The disadvantages of electric cars compared to those with combustion engines remain. For one thing, the cost of a hybrid like the Chevy Volt, which exceeds the clean air standards, is too high for many Americans. There are still no easy solutions for problems like recharging the battery of an electric car while driving around in the city, either. To help make hybrids and fully electric cars more appealing to buyers, the federal government offers financial

A logo on the back of a Nissan LEAF shows it to be a zero emission vehicle (ZEV), meaning it creates no exhaust. California has offered automakers incentives to create more ZEVs in order to improve air quality in the state.

incentives, or cash credits, to people who buy cars that pollute less. In 2011, for example, the government offered a tax credit of $7,500 to buyers of cars such as the Chevy Volt or the Nissan LEAF to help make them more affordable. The state of California, recognizing that inconvenience is one reason why people avoid buying all-electric ZEVs, is also working on making changes to its cities and roadways, such as adding stations for recharging vehicle batteries. As plug-in hybrids and fully electric cars become more commonplace, so will charging stations across the nation. Eventually, this will remove some of the barriers to owning an electric vehicle. If buyers can be encouraged to choose electric cars over those with internal combustion engines, a major source of air pollution could be eliminated, and the country will depend less on fossil fuels.

Not the Only Answer

Vehicles that run completely on battery power may be an improvement over those with internal combustion engines in many ways, but they are not the only answer to problems like air pollution. Electric vehicles still need to be hooked up to a power source in order to have their batteries charged. Plugging an electric car into a wall outlet for several hours every night increases a home's use of electricity, and the electrical power provided to people's homes and businesses also comes mostly from the burning of fossil fuels, such as coal. In the United States, more than half of electrical power plants burn coal to generate electricity, and these plants are major air polluters themselves. If all gasoline-powered vehicles were replaced by electric vehicles, millions of people would be plugging their cars in every night, and that would require more burning of coal to help meet the increase in electricity demands. Fossil fuels would still be depleted, and

Two T-shaped lithium-ion batteries that power the Chevy Volt await installation at a General Motors assembly plant. A potential problem created by the increased popularity of electric cars involves battery disposal.

pollution, in the form of burning coal, would only increase. For these reasons, electric cars are an imperfect solution to the problems of air pollution and dependence on fossil fuels.

Another disadvantage to modern electric cars is that batteries require materials that must be mined. Currently, most stores of the metals used to create lithium-ion batteries like the one used in the Chevy Volt and the Nissan LEAF come from China, where a majority of the batteries are also built before being exported to places like the United States. A shift from gasoline-fueled vehicles to electric ones may only mean that Americans would be trading dependence on countries that produce fossil fuels for dependence on countries that produce batteries. Mined metals are also a

Batteries Gone Bad

In 2006, millions of laptop computers with lithium-ion batteries were recalled for safety reasons. Some users reported cases of batteries swelling, exploding, and causing fires. Manufacturers of the batteries looked into the problem and discovered that if a particle of metal got inside the battery's outer casing while it was being made, the particle could pierce the sheets of lithium that are meant to be kept separate inside the battery. If these metal sheets touch each other, they can begin to react very quickly, raising the heat inside the battery and causing its shell to rupture. Battery manufacturers have worked ever since to improve the safety of batteries in devices like computers and cell phones. Statistically, fewer than one in a million batteries ever have a problem. Now that cars are being made with lithium-ion batteries in them, however, a battery that explodes spontaneously or after being crushed or pierced during a collision could be deadly. Electric automobile makers therefore engineer special protections to keep the battery safe during a crash. Electric vehicle advocates point out that cars have always carried tanks of gasoline, a substance well known for its tendency to explode in a crash, and that battery-powered cars may actually be a safer option.

nonrenewable resource, and supplies of these metals could someday become scarce as well. There is also the problem of disposing of spent batteries. The batteries traditionally used in ignition systems of cars with internal combustion engines have been lead acid batteries, and lead is toxic to the environment when the batteries are disposed of improperly in garbage dumps. Batteries used to power most modern hybrid and electric vehicles are nickel metal hydride and lithium-ion batteries, both of which are thought to be far less damaging to the environment than lead batteries. Nevertheless, if millions of battery-operated vehicles are one day driving around, there is concern that mountains of spent batteries might create a new pollution hazard in the form of toxic waste materials. Companies that manufacture battery-powered cars already have been active in stressing the need for drivers to return spent batteries to the company so their metals can be recycled and any toxic parts neutralized. Since battery-powered cars are still new, however, there is uncertainty about the impact that millions of spent car batteries could begin to have on the environment.

Despite concerns about continuing sources of pollution and where batteries will come from in the future, electric vehicles are still considered a positive choice for the environment. The amount of fossil fuels that must be burned to provide power to recharge an electric car is far less than the amount of gasoline that must be burned to run an internal combustion engine. If all internal combustion engines in the United States were replaced by electric motors, the demand for coal at power plants *would* increase—but these power plants would still burn far less fuel overall than millions of internal combustion engines currently do. Using electricity to recharge car batteries is a much more efficient use of fossil fuels. Scientists are also experimenting with other possibilities besides batteries for providing vehicles with power. "There is no reason not to use our capacity for technological innovation to reduce our dependency on oil decisively—while avoiding fantasies of finding a single perfect solution,"[25] say Woolsey and Sexton. In the search for better solutions, if not perfect ones, innovation in electric vehicle technology could mean that cars may one day be driven without any reliance on fossil fuels at all.

CHAPTER 5

Electric Transportation: The Road to the Future

Whether powered by electricity or combustible fuel, automated vehicles are important machines. They provide people with a ready and reliable means of transportation anywhere and anytime. The ability for people to own and drive a car has become almost essential to participating in the modern American lifestyle. "The car has been seen as a freedom machine...ask any American teenager with a newly issued license," says history professor John A. Heitman. "For most Americans, the automobile is also seen as an absolute necessity. For a senior citizen, the loss of driving privileges is staggering. For a working adult, access to the automobile is often critical to get to the job and back home."[26] Having access to a car allows a person to get around in a country that has been built for automobiles. For many people in the United States, driving a car has become almost as important to individual and family lifestyles as having a home, and changing the kind of cars Americans are used to driving is almost like asking them to change the kind of homes they live in. A switch to electric cars will take years if not decades and could require a total shift in the way Americans think about transportation. Gone may be the days when people toured the country by car for the sheer

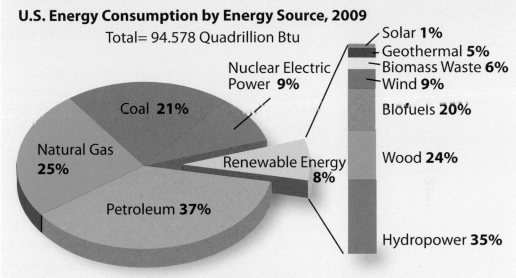

RENEWABLE ENERGY IN THE UNITED STATES

In 2009, eight percent of U.S. energy consumption came from renewable resources like solar power, wind power, and biomass.

U.S. Energy Consumption by Energy Source, 2009

Total= 94.578 Quadrillion Btu

Solar **1%**
Geothermal **5%**
Biomass Waste **6%**
Wind **9%**
Biofuels **20%**
Wood **24%**
Hydropower **35%**

Nuclear Electric Power **9%**

Coal **21%**

Natural Gas **25%**

Petroleum **37%**

Renewable Energy **8%**

Note: Sum of components may not equal 100% due to independent rounding.

Source: Data taken from "Energy Sources: Renewable." Energy Kids (U.S. Energy Information Administration). www.eia.doe.gov/kids/energy.cfm?page=renewable_home#tab2

pleasure of driving, for example—battery-powered cars may not be able to carry people so many miles from home anymore. Drivers would have to start thinking about efficiency and necessity rather than just driving for fun. Towns, cities, and even people's homes would start to look different, too, with charging stations replacing street-corner gas stations and with powerful charging outlets added to garages, driveways, and parking spaces in apartment buildings. The payoffs, however, would be significant. American dependence on foreign oil would be greatly reduced, and the air would be fresher, especially in big cities.

Of course, demand for electric power would be at an all-time high as millions of Americans charged their cars every

BITS & BYTES

1.5 million

Number of barrels of oil it would take to create as much energy as 0.4 mi^2 (1km^2) of desert receives from the sun in a year

night for use the next day. The nation would still rely on a dwindling supply of fossil fuels, and coal-burning plants would still be polluting the atmosphere. Environmentalists and economists see electric cars like the Nissan LEAF as a great improvement over internal combustion engines, but the cars of the future may be different entirely. Inventors are seeking new ways to use technology to end human dependence on fossil fuels altogether. The automobiles of the future may be powered by *renewable* sources of energy, resources that are in abundant supply on Earth and always will be.

The Sun as Fuel

When looking for ways to power an electricity-dependent human lifestyle, it makes sense to look to the sky. The sun's light and heat are basic, constant sources of energy for the planet. As long as the sun shines, its energy can be captured and converted into the kind of energy that can do work—such as the mechanical energy needed to make a car's motor, axles, and wheels turn. Solar power, energy that comes from the sun, has long been touted as a possible way to provide the electricity that can make automobiles function, and this idea is gaining more notice as the years go by. "Right now solar is such a small fraction of U.S. electricity production that it's measured in tenths of a percent," says Robert Hawsey, an associate director of the U.S. National Renewable Energy Laboratory. "But that's expected to grow. Ten to 20 percent of the nation's peak electricity demand could be provided by solar energy by 2030."[27] Some of that energy could even be harnessed on the roofs of cars simply by equipping them with solar cells.

These solar cells, also called photovoltaic cells, are devices that capture light energy and turn it into electricity, or volts. Certain substances have photoelectric properties—when they are exposed to light energy, the light splits electrons

The Venturi Eclectic is equipped with solar panels that capture light energy from the sun in order to provide the vehicle with power. The use of solar power in the United States is expected to increase over the coming decades.

apart from the atoms in the substance. If a flat panel of the photoelectric substance is connected to positively and negatively charged surfaces to form an electrical circuit, these floating electrons can be channeled into an electric current. If multiple solar cells are combined into larger panels, the electric current they produce can be used to do work like power an electric motor in a car.

Automobiles with onboard solar panels on their roofs are already being manufactured to take advantage of the sun. Some models look like giant tables with wheels instead of legs and a small hole in the middle where a driver can sit and steer. Others more closely resemble a typical passenger car. The Venturi Eclectic is a tiny automobile that seats one or two people and can drive about five miles when fully charged with solar energy. The REVA NXR is a bigger solar car that can seat four people. Using energy from large solar panels

Swifter than the Sun

Vehicles that can travel on the power of sunlight alone are still something of a rarity, but among engineering students at colleges and universities worldwide, certain solar cars have become well known. Most famous of these is the Sunswift IVy, a true "hot rod" among solar vehicles. Early in 2011, the table-shaped, one-passenger car toppled a world record for the fastest average speed a solar vehicle has ever maintained while completing two 500-meter (0.3 mile) racing courses with just an hour to recharge in between. The Sunswift IVy kept up an average speed of 55 mph (89 kph) to break the previous record of 49 mph (78 kph) per hour, set in 1988 by the General Motors Sunraycer. The Sunswift IVy also took first place in the 2009 World Solar Challenge, an 1,800-mile (3,000km) electric-car race across Australia. With a top speed of 72 mph (115 kph), the Sunswift IVy is the latest leader of solar-powered cars. Unfortunately, its $280,000 price tag makes mass production unlikely. It could, however, be an ancestor to affordable solar cars of the future.

on its roof, the REVA NXR can travel about 15 miles (24km) when fully charged.

On a sunny day, cars like these could be useful for people who only need to travel a few miles at a time, such as to a neighborhood supermarket and back home again. For solar power to be a realistic option for most drivers, though, solar cells would have to be much more efficient at capturing energy. In addition, they would have to be able to provide enough power to drive at least 30 miles (48km) between charges. Most current photovoltaic cells capture only about one-fifth of the available energy in the sun's rays and convert it to electricity. Until more efficient solar cells are developed, solar-powered cars may not be practical for many drivers. In cloudy climates, such as the Pacific Northwest of the United States, which averages only about seventy sunny days a year, solar vehicles rarely would have enough charge to go anywhere.

Wind as Power

Where the sun does not shine, however, the wind often blows. Wind is another natural resource that is completely renewable. It can be used to turn turbines, which are like pinwheels. As wind blows against the angled spokes of the turbine, they spin, and the motion can be captured and converted into electrical energy. The solar-powered Venturi Eclectic also has an optional turbine that can be clipped on so that a mix of sun and wind energy can help power the car. As with solar energy, though, wind energy is practical only in certain places—those where the wind frequently blows. The solar-powered Eclectic, with a top speed of 30 miles (48km) per hour, often drives too slowly for wind resistance to fully power the vehicle while it is in motion.

Cars with built-in mechanisms to capture solar and wind power are not likely to be practical replacements for gasoline or battery-powered vehicles anytime soon. Electricity created by solar or wind energy, however, can be generated at large power plants and transported along power lines to other locations, where it can be used to charge car batteries. Coal-burning power plants could be supplemented by others

Wind turbines and solar panels capture energy that can be converted to electricity. Such sources of renewable energy could be used to power charging stations for electric cars.

that get energy from the sun and the wind. All three sources could work together to make the electricity that powers things like electric cars. Smaller roadside solar and wind plants can also be built to provide charging stations where a few electric vehicles at a time could stop, plug in, and have their batteries recharged with electricity from the sun or the wind. There is a solar recharging station in Brooklyn, New York, for this purpose already.

Hybrid and fully electric cars are also being developed in which solar and wind power are used to supplement the car's main battery. Power from the sun and wind can perform low-energy functions such as cooling and heating the car, rather than the larger task of making the car move. Such energy-saving devices could help keep cars comfortable for passengers while not affecting the range they can be driven on one battery charge. Solar power and wind are just some of the renewable-energy options that could help provide some of the power needs for electric cars in the future. "These cars are not going to be suitable for everyone," says electric vehicle retailer and enthusiast Michael Boxwell, "yet the first exciting steps towards practical solar road cars have been made. With the advancement of solar panels with better capacities and lower costs and the ongoing development of electric cars, it may not be that long before solar electric cars become a common sight on our roads."[28]

Driving on Garbage

The sun and wind are not the only renewable resources that can be used to create electricity. The world also has an abundant supply of another potential fuel source—garbage. The amount of waste that human beings throw away is increasing along with the human population. The average American tosses out 4.5 pounds (2kg) of garbage a day, about double the amount of waste that was produced by the average American in the 1960s. A majority of that garbage is gathered from streets within towns and cities and trucked to landfills to be dumped. As people produce more garbage, the world's dumping sites only get larger and more numerous.

There is an alternative use for much of what people throw away, however. Much of the material that gets tossed is plant and animal waste, called biomass. Plants and animals contain energy-rich carbon molecules, and when they die, these molecules can be broken apart to release energy in the form of heat. Fossil fuels are essentially stores of dead plant and animal matter that has been compressed and fossilized over millions of years. Biomass is a store of plant and animal matter that died much more recently. When it is burned, biomass releases energy, just like when coal or gasoline is burned. Whereas biomass takes millions of years to fossilize, liquefy, and become crude oil that is burned for energy, the energy from burning biomass itself is available immediately.

Burning biomass for energy is not a new idea. For thousands of years, humans have burned wood in fireplaces for

Electric Delivery

For residents of Petaluma, California, having packages delivered to their business or home became much more economical in 2009. The Petaluma branch of the United Parcel Service (UPS) added about forty ZAP Xebras to its delivery fleet. These three-wheeled, pickup-style electric vehicles carry less cargo than a UPS van, but they use no fuel and emit no exhaust. They are quiet, too, unlike the boxy brown UPS vans heard rumbling through the neighborhoods of other towns and cities. The Xebra can travel up to 40 miles on a single charge of its battery and can reach a maximum speed of 45 miles (72km) per hour, making it an ideal vehicle for transporting packages from a local distribution center to people's doorsteps. At an affordable cost of about $10,000 apiece, Xebras are in a position to save parcel delivery companies like UPS a lot of money while also helping to preserve the environment. Mail-order customers nationwide may soon see (but not hear or smell) more electric vehicles delivering their packages. Parcel delivery is one task for which the electric vehicle is perfectly suited.

A ZAP Xebra electric car joins the traditional brown truck as parts of United Parcel Service's (UPS) delivery fleet in Petaluma, California.

heat and as a means to cook food. Today, a lot of biomass can be sorted out of landfills and sent to power plants where it can be burned to heat water and create steam, which turns huge turbines that provide electricity. Biomass crops can even be grown for the purpose of being burned later for energy. Although burning biomass does release smoke and carbon dioxide into the atmosphere, trees and plants also draw carbon dioxide out of the atmosphere during the process of photosynthesis, in which plants use sunlight and carbon dioxide to make their own food. The carbon dioxide put into the atmosphere from burning biomass, therefore, is thought to be balanced out by the carbon dioxide recently taken out of the atmosphere if new biomass crops are being grown nearby. This balance is not achieved when fossil fuels are burned, because the plant matter from which they were formed has not taken carbon dioxide out of the atmosphere for a very long time. "Fossil fuels are derived from plants and animals that had lived millions of years back" and took thousands of years to grow in the first place, say environmental engineers Tasneem Abassi and S.A. Abassi. "We have released (and are continuing to release) enormous quantities

A bulldozer moves woodchips used as fuel at a power plant in Sweden. Woodchips and other waste from plants and animals, known as biomass, can be burned for energy.

of CO_2 within a very short time of about 200 years. For this reason, it can be said that fossil fuels are 'carbon-positive.' Biomass, on the other hand, is 'carbon-neutral.' Its use as fuel only [releases] that much CO_2 which had been captured from the biomass during its growth."[29] Unlike burning fossil fuels for energy, growing new plants to burn as biomass helps keep carbon dioxide levels in check and causes little to no net increase in the world's carbon dioxide pollution.

Biomass-fueled power plants are one more possibility for creating the additional electricity society will need as more people make a shift to electric cars. Electricity works the same way, no matter how it is created—whether by renewable sources like sun, wind, and biomass, or by nonrenewable resources like the burning of coal. Finding new ways to generate power so that electric cars can be plugged into outlets and recharged will help reduce the world's dependence on fossil fuels. In the case of biomass, new stores of energy could be as close as the nearest landfill. Cars of the future might run on electricity from a mix of sources like sun, wind, and biomass. Power will just be created at power plants and transferred to a battery instead of being generated within the vehicle itself as internal combustion engines do. "Electricity is transportable— it can be generated at a low-cost location and conveniently shipped hundreds of miles to where it is needed," says electrical engineer Bob Brant. "A storage battery, charged from electricity provided by a convenient wall outlet, can reliably carry electricity to start a car anywhere, or power an electric vehicle."[30] The portable nature of electricity and the variety of ways it can be generated provide exciting new possibilities for electric cars and the energy sources that will power them.

A New Kind of Fuel

Most electric vehicles depend on this "transportable" energy that is created somewhere else (at a power plant), delivered to the car through a power outlet, and stored in the car's battery until it needs to be used. These cars have no need for a fuel tank that must be regularly refilled. There is one kind of electric car, however, that does carry a supply of fuel onboard. That fuel is hydrogen gas, one of the important elements

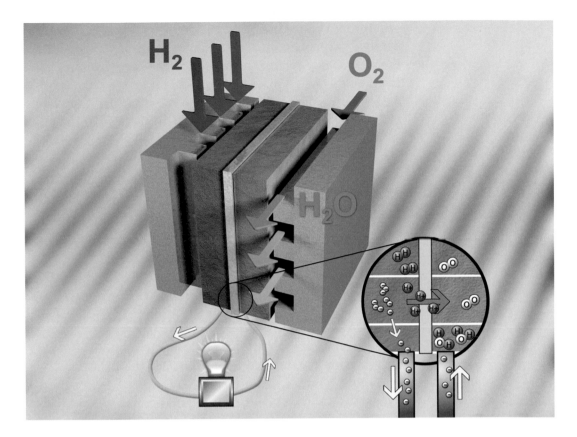

in fuel cells, devices that convert energy from fuel, such as electrical energy from hydrogen gas. In a car, electrical energy from a fuel cell can run an electric motor. Hydrogen fuel cells are one of the newest technological inventions available for powering a vehicle. They require no burning of fossil fuels, either within the car's engine or at a power plant far away, and the only emissions they release into the environment are heat and water.

Hydrogen fuel cells work something like batteries. They split negatively charged electrons from other molecules and channel the negative charge to generate electricity. Unlike most batteries, however, which require metallic substances that chemically react with each other, fuel cells need only two things to create energy: hydrogen gas and oxygen from the air itself. A hydrogen molecule (H) is very small, containing only one positively charged proton in its nucleus, which is orbited by one negatively charged electron. The fuel cell contains a catalyst, a substance that starts a chemical

A diagram shows how hydrogen fuel cells work. Hydrogen is pumped into the cell (red arrows), where the negatively charged electrons in the nuclei (dark blue) are split from the protons (yellow). The electrons pass through a circuit to create electricity.

reaction but does not get consumed in that reaction. The catalyst, when it comes into contact with hydrogen, splits the negatively charged electrons of the hydrogen atoms apart from the protons in their nuclei. The negatively charged electrons are then channeled through a circuit to produce electricity, which can power a car's motor. When the electrons complete their passage through the circuit, they reunite with the hydrogen protons. Meanwhile, the fuel cell draws oxygen molecules (O_2) from the surrounding air. These oxygen molecules combine with the electrons and protons of the hydrogen molecules, forming a new substance with two hydrogen molecules for every oxygen molecule. The result is H_2O, or water. This and heat are the only by-products that fuel cells release to the atmosphere. Fuel cells require no fossil fuels and no electricity, just compressed hydrogen gas. They power a quiet, efficient electric motor while producing no air pollution at all.

Cars powered by fuel cells are on the road already. The Honda Motor Company manufactures the FCX Clarity, a four-door family sedan powered entirely by hydrogen fuel

Becoming an Electric Vehicle Engineer

Job Description: Electric vehicle engineers develop the electrical systems and mechanical parts that work together beneath an electric car's hood. Their responsibilities may include designing electrical circuits, wiring the car's systems, and packaging electrical components so they work safely and reliably.

Education: This job requires a minimum of an undergraduate degree in electrical and/or automotive engineering, with coursework in electronic systems.

Qualifications: Many employers prefer candidates who have a professional engineering license or certification, which usually requires special coursework and a passing score on an exam.

Additional Information: There is growing demand for engineers specializing in the relatively new field of electric vehicles. Car manufacturers are producing more electric cars and need engineers who specialize in the mechanics of cars and electrical technology equally. Electric vehicle engineers require good teamwork skills and must work well under pressure.

Salary: $55,000 to more than $80,000 a year

cells. The FCX Clarity has a tank that stores pressurized hydrogen gas and a fuel cell to convert the hydrogen into electricity before binding it with oxygen taken from the air outside the vehicle. The electricity created by the fuel cell powers an electric motor that drives the car. The FCX Clarity also has a battery that stores extra energy created from the fuel cell and from the car's regenerative braking system. The FCX Clarity can drive about 240 miles (386km) before its tank needs to be refilled with pressurized hydrogen. Refueling takes only a few minutes, similar to refilling a gasoline tank but unlike the hours it takes to recharge the battery in other electric vehicles. Because its motor is electric, the FCX Clarity operates as quietly as any other electric car, and the water it produces as its only by-product is said to be pure enough to drink.

The hydrogen-powered Honda FCX Clarity is offered for sale only in Southern California, where a few hydrogen filling stations can be found.

The Drawbacks of Fuel Cells

Electric cars powered by hydrogen fuel cells seem like a promising alternative to internal combustion for the future. Fuel-cell technology is not without safety concerns, however.

Hydrogen gas must be highly compressed in order to be stored in a tank and used as fuel. The pressure within a car's hydrogen storage tank can make it dangerous—if the vehicle is in a collision, the tank could potentially explode and cause serious injuries to passengers or people standing nearby. There is also concern that hydrogen tanks may have a potential to leak. Hydrogen is flammable, so if hydrogen gas were to leak into the passenger space of a car and be exposed to a spark or other ignition source, the car might explode. Because hydrogen fuel-cell vehicles are a new invention and very few of them yet exist, future studies must be done to determine whether fuel cells are any more or less dangerous than cars with onboard gasoline tanks.

In addition to the potential safety risks of fuel-cell vehicles like the FCX Clarity, perhaps an even greater downside is that society is not yet prepared for this technology. The compressed hydrogen that provides electricity for the car can be produced by burning natural gas, but few companies do so because fuel-cell technology is still very new. Therefore, hydrogen refueling stations are so rare that the Honda FCX Clarity cannot be driven anywhere except Southern California, where a few hydrogen refueling stations do exist. For this reason, Honda offers the FCX Clarity only to California customers. When it introduced the car in 2010, Honda produced just 200 of the vehicles, and these could not be purchased. Customers could only lease them for 36 months at a cost of $600 per month.

Fuel-cell technology is so new that most Americans are unaware the FCX Clarity even exists. Nevertheless, Honda is hopeful that its fuel-cell vehicle could soon become a true competitor in the automobile market. "Honda has brought the fuel cell vehicle from the lab to the fleet and finally to the public," the company's website says. "The major barrier now is building up the hydrogen supply infrastructure."[31] If and when that happens, hydrogen vehicles could eventually replace gasoline-powered cars, reduce America's dependence on foreign oil, and eliminate a major source of air pollution, all without making major changes to the way people live and drive. Newer ways of producing compressed hydrogen gas using renewable resources like solar and wind power could make fuel-cell electric vehicles even more environmentally friendly. Fuel cells could be the technology that stands behind electric automobiles of the future.

A World with No Gasoline

The world is making a slow shift to electric vehicles, whether they are powered by rechargeable batteries, the sun, the wind, hydrogen fuel cells, or some other technology not yet invented. Though the gasoline-powered engine is still the popular choice of vehicles in the United States, rising oil prices and pressure from world governments for countries to scale back on air pollution may soon bring about the last days of internal combustion. Electric automobiles, however, are poised to take on the task of transporting people easily and conveniently where they need to go. "The long-term

A car is plugged in for a recharge, a sight that is expected to become increasingly familiar in the coming years as more people choose to drive electric vehicles.

future of car transportation is among all likelihood electric, as electricity has many advantages as a fuel substitute,"[32] says microbiologist Alain A. Vertés.

The shift to electric vehicles will not happen overnight, especially in places like the United States, where society has largely revolved around the needs and abilities of internal combustion engines for so long. People will have to change the way they think about driving, and perhaps even the way they live—speed limits may be reduced to maximize the efficiency of electric cars, for example, and more people may have to get used to charging their cars in their garages at home rather than planning to quickly refuel at the corner gas station on their way to wherever they are going. There will be benefits, too—breathable air, quieter streets and freeways, a lower cost of driving, and less worry about where and how America will get its crude oil in the future. "The really encouraging thing about the electric car is that these are still its early days," says Jamie Kitman, a columnist for *Automobile* magazine. "The internal-combustion engine has had 125 years to become the much-improved but still imperfect device it is today; we've just started to focus on investing in the technology of electric engines. For electric cars, the game has just begun."[33] Electric cars were once as popular as internal combustion engines. After more than a century of roadways dominated by gasoline-powered cars, it is getting easier to imagine a future where electric cars may take a quiet and clean lead once again.

NOTES

Chapter 1:
Electric Vehicles, Past to Present

1. Hans Camenzind. *Much Ado about Almost Nothing: Man's Encounter with the Electron.* Bangor, ME: Booklocker.com, Inc., 2007, p. 30.
2. Michael Dooley. *The Great Horseless Carriage Race.* New York: Holiday House, 2002, p. 30.
3. William Pelfrey. *Billy, Alfred, and General Motors: The Story of Two Unique Men, a Legendary Company, and a Remarkable Time in American History.* New York: AMACOM, 2006, p. 166.
4. Curtis Darrell Anderson and Judy Anderson. *Electric and Hybrid Cars: A History.* Jefferson, NC: McFarland & Company, 2010, p. 3.
5. Anderson and Anderson. *Electric and Hybrid Cars,* p. 4.
6. Bob Brant. *Build Your Own Electric Vehicle.* Blue Ridge Summit, PA: TAB Books, 1994, p. 6.

Chapter 2:
Under the Hood of a Car

7. V. Ganesan. *Internal Combustion Engines.* 3rd ed. New Delhi: Tata McGraw-Hill, 2008, p. 1.
8. Tom Philbin. *The 100 Greatest Inventions of All Time: A Ranking Past and Present.* New York: Citadel Press Books, 2003, p. 31.
9. Brant. *Build Your Own Electric Vehicle,* p. 214.
10. John C. Kotz, Paul Treichel, and John Raymond Townsend. *Chemistry and Chemical Reactivity, Vol. 2.* 7th ed. Belmont, CA: Thomson Higher Education, 2009, p. 915.

Chapter 3:
The Hybrid and the Electric Revolution

11. Kotz, Treichel, and Townsend. *Chemistry and Chemical Reactivity,* p. 915.
12. Michael Boxwell. *Owning an Electric Car: 2010 Edition.* Warwickshire, UK: Greenstream Publishing, 2010, pp. 18–19.

13. Quoted in Sharon Silke Carty. "Bob Lutz, GM's New Image Chief, Says He'll 'Tell It Like It Is.'" *USA Today*, July 15, 2009. www.usatoday.com/money/autos/2009-07-14-gm-image-lutz_N.htm.

14. General Motors Company. "Hybrids That Fit the Way You Live." www.chevrolet.com/pages/open/default/fuel/hybrid.do.

15. Quoted in HybridCars.com. "GM's Lutz: 80% Vehicles Will Be Hybrids by 2020." March 19, 2008. www.hybridcars.com/news/lutz-hybrids-will-be-one-third-gm-sales-2015.html.

16. Quoted at the Chevrolet website. www.chevrolet.com/volt.

17. Quoted at the Chevrolet website. www.chevrolet.com/volt.

18. Quoted in "Reservation Plans." Nissan USA. www.nissanusa.com/leaf-electric-car/index?dcp=ppn.39666654.&dcc=0.216878497#/leaf-electric-car/video/all/it_all_started_on_Tour/reservation_plans.

Chapter 4: Electric Cars in the Modern World

19. Gijs Mom. *The Electric Vehicle: Technology and Expectations in the Automobile Age*. Baltimore, MD: Johns Hopkins University Press, 2004, pp. 1–2.

20. U.S. Environmental Protection Agency. "Human-Related Sources and Sinks of Carbon Dioxide." www.epa.gov/climatechange/emissions/co2_human.html.

21. Clarke E. Cochran, Lawrence C. Mayer, T. R. Carr, and N. Joseph Cayer. *American Public Policy: An Introduction*. 9th ed. Boston, MA: Wadsworth Cengage Learning, 2009, p. 114.

22. Quoted in Steve Connor. "Warning: Oil Supplies Are Running Out Fast." *The Independent*, August 3, 2009. www.independent.co.uk/news/science/warning-oil-supplies-are-running-out-fast-1766585.html.

23. R. James Woolsey and Chelsea Sexton. "Geopolitical Implications of Plug-in Vehicles." In *Plug-in Electric Vehicles: What Role for Washington?*, edited by David B. Sandalow. Washington, DC: Brookings Institution, 2009, p. 18.

24. California Environmental Protection Agency Air Resources Board. "Zero Emission Vehicle (ZEV) Program." www.arb.ca.gov/msprog/zevprog/zevprog.htm.

25. Woolsey and Sexton. "Geopolitical Implications of Plug-in Vehicles," p. 20.

Chapter Five: Electric Transportation: The Road to the Future

26. John A. Heitman. *The Autombobile and American Life*. Jefferson, NC: McFarland & Company, 2009, p. 3.

27. Quoted in George Johnson. "Plugging Into the Sun." *National Geographic*, September 2009.

http://ngm.nationalgeographic
.com/2009/09/solar/johnson-text/1.

28. Boxwell. *Owning an Electric Car*,
p. 179.

29. Tasneem Abassi and S. A. Abassi.
*Renewable Energy Sources: Their
Impact on Global Warming and
Pollution.* New Delhi, India: PHI
Private Learning Ltd., 2010, p. 57.

30. Brant. *Build Your Own Electric
Vehicle*, p. 34.

31. American Honda Motor Company.
"FCX Clarity." http://automobiles
.honda.com/fcx-clarity/.

32. Alain A. Vertés. "Axes of Development
in Chemical Process Engineering
for Converting Biomass to Energy."
In *Biomass to Biofuels: Strategies for
Global Industries*, edited by Alain A.
Vertés, Hideaki Yukawa, and Hans
P. Blaschek. Chichester, UK: John
Wiley & Sons, 2010, p. 512.

33. Quoted in "Can Electric Cars Make a
Go of It?" *The New York Times Upfront*,
January 29, 2011. http://teacher.
scholastic.com/scholasticnews/
indepth/upfront/debate/index
.asp?article=d013111.

acid: A chemical substance whose molecules have a strong tendency to react (exchange electrons with) molecules of other substances.

battery: A device that produces an electric current by harnessing the chemical reactions that take place within its compartments, or cells.

biomass: Plant and animal waste products that can be burned to release energy.

combustion: A rapid chemical process that produces heat and usually light; the act of burning.

crude oil: A slick, flammable liquid mixture of hydrogen and carbon that can be refined into other materials, such as gasoline; also called petroleum.

electrical energy: Energy made available by the flow of an electrical charge.

electricity: A form of energy that is based on the movement and interaction of tiny charged particles called electrons.

electrolyte: A substance that conducts electricity.

electromagnet: A device made of an iron or steel core and wrapped with wire; when an electrical current passes through the wire, the device becomes magnetic, with the ability to attract iron or steel.

engine: A machine that converts thermal (heat) energy into mechanical force or motion.

fuel cell: An electrochemical device that converts energy from a fuel, such as hydrogen, into electrical energy.

hybrid: Any vehicle that uses two or more sources of power.

internal combustion engine: A device that uses heat energy created within the engine itself, through small, controlled explosions, to move a piston and create mechanical energy.

mechanical energy: Energy that moves objects, such as the wheels of a car.

motor: Machine that converts electrical energy into mechanical force or motion.

nonrenewable resource: A natural resource that cannot be regrown or regenerated, either at all or quickly enough to match the rate at which humans use it.

photovoltaic cell: A device that converts solar energy into electric energy.

regenerative brake: A mechanical device that reduces a vehicle's speed by changing some of the wheels' energy into electricity instead of releasing the energy into the atmosphere as heat.

renewable resource: A natural resource that can be replaced naturally at the same rate as it is used by humans.

steam engine: A device that uses an external heat source to turn water to steam, which moves a turbine or a piston to create mechanical energy.

torque: A measure of the force available in a twisting or rotating motion, such as the turning of a wheel.

voltage: A measure of electric force, such as that which can be created in a battery.

Books

Stephanie Bearce. *All About Electric and Hybid Cars and Who's Driving Them.* Tell Your Parents series, Hockessin, DE: Mitchell Lane, 2009. This book explains what electric and hybrid cars are, why they are becoming more popular, and some of the advantages that might make a person want to own one.

James Billmaier. *JOLT! The Impending Dominance of the Electric Car and Why America Must Take Charge.* Charleston, SC: Advantage, 2010. An inventor and electric car advocate explains why gasoline-powered vehicles are a burden on America and how electric vehicles can fix the problem.

Richard Hammond. *Car Science: An Under-the-Hood, Behind-the-Dash Look at How Cars Work.* New York: Dorling Kindersley Children, 2008. This reader-friendly book gives a history of automobile technology and explains the workings of all kinds of automobiles, including new electric vehicle technology and possible cars of the future.

Arvid Linde. *Electric Cars the Future Is Now! Your Guide to the Cars You Can Buy Now and What the Future Holds.* Dorchester, UK: Veloce Publishing, 2010. Readers will learn the basics of how electric cars are built and how they work, as well as how they fit into the modern world and what their role will be in the future.

Jack R. Nerad. *The Complete Idiot's Guide to Hybrid and Alternative Fuel Vehicles.* New York: Alpha Books, 2007. Various examples of modern hybrid and electric vehicles are described, along with how they work, their advantages, and their disadvantages.

Saddleback Educational Publishing. *Alternative Fuels*, Think Green series. Irvine, CA: Saddleback Educational Publishing, 2009. Many alternatives to fossil fuels are discussed in this book, including solar and wind energy and biomass. There are also chapters on electric and hybrid vehicles.

Articles

Frances Romero. "A Brief History of the Electric Car." *Time*, January 13, 2009. www.time.com/time/business/article/0,8599,1871282,00.html. This article discusses the past—and the growing future—of electric car technology.

"The Future of Filling Up." *National Geographic*, October 15, 2009. http://ngm.nationalgeographic.com/big-idea/04/electric-cars. This illustrated special feature gives an overview of changes that modern cities will have to make to support the growing number of electric cars that is expected in the future.

Websites

U.S. Environmental Protection Agency: Electric Vehicles (www.fueleconomy.gov/feg/evtech.shtml). This site, presented by the EPA's Energy Efficiency & Renewable Energy unit, provides information about current and upcoming electric vehicles, where to find them, government incentives to buy and drive one, information on alternative fuels, and more.

Energy Kids (www.eia.doe.gov/kids/). Presented by the U.S. Energy Information Association, this site includes facts, games, activities, calculators, and much more to help answer questions about energy. The website includes a special section on electric transportation.

Popular Science: Cars (www.popsci.com/cars). The website of *Popular Science* magazine provides continuously updated information on new car technology, models of electric and hybrid vehicles, and more.

INDEX

Fossil fuels
    electric vehicles, 71–72, 73
    environmental issues, 61–64
    formation, *65*
    petroleum supply, 64–68
Four-stroke cylinder, 33–35
Franklin, Benjamin, 12–13, *14*
Fuel cells, 84–89, *85*
Full-size hybrids, *51*, 51–53

G
Galvani, Luigi, 13–14
Garbage, 81, 83–84
Gas mileage
    hybrid vehicles, 50–51, 53
    Toyota Prius, 48
Gasoline, 24, 31–32
    cost, 67–68
    hybrid vehicles, 53
Gasoline-powered generators, 55
Generators, 55
Global warming, 64

H
Honda Civic Hybrid, 50
Honda FCX Clarity, 86–87, *87*, 88
Hong Kong, China, 62
Hybrid vehicles, *47*
    advantages, 50–51
    celebrities, use by, 46, *46*
    disadvantages, 51–54
    technology, 46–48
    Toyota Prius, 48–50, *49*
Hydrogen fuel cells, 84–89, *85*, *87*

I
Incentives, government, 70–71
Infrastructure, 88–89
Internal combustion engines, *30*
    advantages and disadvantages,
      21–22

chemistry, 36–37
effects of, 11, *11*
electric cars' advantages over, 44
environmental issues, 61–64
fuel, 31–32
lead acid batteries, 40–41
lifestyle issues, 68–70
mechanics of, 32–35, *33*
Model T, *25*
popularity, 23–27, 30–31,
    35–36, 45
Inventions
    automobiles, 10
    batteries, 14–16
    diesel engines, 34
    electric ignition, 25–27
    internal combustion engine, 32
    street-sized vehicle, 20

K
Kettering, Charles, 26

L
Lead acid batteries, 16, 40–42
LEAF, Nissan, 56–58, *57*, 63
Lightning, 12–13
Lithium-ion batteries, *41*, *66*, *71*
    lead acid batteries, as replacements
      for, 41, 42–43
    mining, 66, 72–73
Locomotive trains, 19, *19*
London, England, 21, *45*, 69
Los Angeles, California, 59, *59*
Lutz, Bob, 52–53

M
Maintenance, 44
Mass transit
    electric vehicles, 28
    subways, 21
    trolleys, *27*, 28

Trucks, 51, *51*, 53
Turbines, 79–81, *80*

U
United Parcel Service (UPS), 82, *82*
United States
   energy consumption, *75*
   lifestyle issues, 68–70
   petroleum supply, 66–67
Urban areas. *See* Cities
Utility companies, 63, 75–76

V
Venturi Eclectic, *77*, 78, 79
Volt, Chevrolet, 54–56, *55*, 63
Volta, Alessandro, 14–15, *16*

W
Wind power, 79–81, *80*

Z
ZAP Xebras, 82, *82*
Zero emission vehicles, *70*, 70–71

PICTURE CREDITS

Cover photo: Wth/Shutterstock.com

andrea lehmkuhl/Shutterstock.com, 89

anweber/Shutterstock.com, 80

AP Images/Chuck Burton, 55

AP Images/PRNewsFoto/ZAP, 82

Bill Pugliano/Getty Images, 71

Charles D. Winters/Photo Researchers, Inc., 66

© ClassicStock/Alamy, 19

© David J. Green–electrical/Alamy, 9 (bottom)

Equinox Graphics/Photo Researchers, Inc., 85

ERIC ESTRADE/AFP/Getty Images, 77

FPG/Getty Images, 30

Gale, Cengage Learning, 17, 41, 47, 49, 65, 75

Getty Images, 25

Hulton Archive/Getty Images, 14

© INTERFOTO/Alamy, 16

© izmostock/Alamy, 9 (top)

© Jon Arnold Images Ltd/Alamy, 59

KAZUHIRO NOGI/AFP/Getty Images, 57

Li Wa/Shutterstock.com, 21

© Mark Scheuern/Alamy, 63

Mark Sullivan/WireImage/Getty Images, 46

Martin Bond/Photo Researchers, Inc., 69

© Mary Evans Picture Library/Alamy, 8 (bottom)

© mediacolor's/Alamy, 8 (top left)

Mike Mergen/Bloomberg via Getty Images, 87

NASA/Photo Researchers, Inc., 62

Rafael Ramirez Lee/Shutterstock.com, 27

© Rob Bartee/Alamy, 31

© Ron Niebrugge/Alamy, 11

Science Source/Photo Researchers, Inc., 34

© sciencephotos/Alamy, 39

© Scott Camazine/Alamy, 36

Sheila Terry/Photo Researchers, Inc., 45

SOREN ANDERSSON/AFP/Getty Images, 83

SSPL/Getty Images, 8 (top right)

Tony Avelar/Bloomberg via Getty Images, 70

© Transtock Inc./Alamy, 51

© Universal Images Group Limited/Alamy, 33

© Vintage Images/Alamy, 22

ABOUT THE AUTHOR

Jenny MacKay is the author of thirteen nonfiction books for middle-grade and teen readers. She lives with her husband, son, and daughter in northern Nevada, where she was born and raised. She is currently trying to figure out how to afford an electric Tesla Roadster sports car.